# First Steps
## to a
# Vegetarian Family

by
**Carole Clement**

## foulsham
LONDON • NEW YORK • TORONTO • SYDNEY

# foulsham

The Publishing House, Bennetts Close,
Cippenham, Berkshire, SL1 5AP, England.

ISBN  0-572-01977-7

Printed in Great Britain by
Cox & Wyman Ltd, Reading, Berkshire.

# CONTENTS

# INTRODUCTION

## First Steps to a Vegetarian Family

We have all recently been made aware that eating too much animal fat can lead to heart disease, cancer and other illnesses. Young children often go through a phase of not liking meat and refuse to eat it. Teenagers and adults learn about the issue of cruelty to animals and show their concern by rejecting animal products. As a result, many people have chosen to turn towards a vegetarian diet. This book gives easy and interesting alternatives to just cutting out meat and introduces nourishing, tasty wholefood equivalents to encourage the whole family to improve their diet.

# A Healthy Balance

Everyone needs to eat foods from the four main food groups every day.

**Protein** for growth, skin and bone repair. Meat and fish are two of the main sources. But others are pulses (dried peas, beans and lentils), cheese, milk, eggs, nuts and vegetable proteins like quorn or tofu. Eat at least two portions a day. Try and make sure children have 600 ml/1 pt/2½ cups milk (including that used in cooking) every day too.

**Carbohydrates** for energy and as fillers. These are found in cereals, bread, pasta and rice. Eat lots every day. They are not fattening - it is only the fat or sugar you put on them which piles on the calories!

**Fats** for body warmth and energy. If you are not eating meat and fish you can get most of what you need in milk, cheese, eggs and nuts. Also from vegetable or nut margarines and oils (but eat sparingly).

**Vitamins and Minerals** for general health and well being. Eat lots of fruit and vegetables in any form (even frozen or canned but preferably without added sugar or salt).

### Note:
Whole milk has a high fat content. Children under two need this for development. Over two give them semi-skimmed milk if they are eating a good, balanced diet (otherwise keep up the whole milk) and over five change to skimmed milk if you prefer.

# Step By Step

It's not difficult to change from a meateating regime to a vegetarian one, but it's not a good idea to do it all at once. A vegetarian diet is high in fibre; however this can be too bulky for young children. So do take it gradually – don't rush into wholefoods all in one go. There is nothing wrong with your children eating white bread if they prefer it or having cornflakes rather than muesli. BUT do try to avoid sugar – it won't do their teeth any good!

## Step 1
To start with, try experimenting with quorn, "vege" mince, dried soya mince or similar textured vegetable protein which looks and tastes just like mince. Substitute it in your favourite mince recipes (with a well–flavoured sauce) and see how the family like it.

## Step 2
Try out the vegetable accompaniments in this book with your normal grills or roasts. Cut vegetables into unusual shapes and sizes to add interest.

## Step 3
Leaf through and pick out a few vegetarian versions of family favourites like burgers, cottage pie, lasagne or moussaka. Just include them on odd days instead of the meat versions.

## Step 4
Gradually give your family more non-meat main courses and accompaniments. Once you've got a repertoire established, say goodbye to meat!

## Note:
This book is not designed for vegans although some of the recipes are suitable.

# Notes on Recipes

* Ingredients are given in metric, Imperial and American. Use only one set in a recipe, do not mix them.

* All spoon measures are level.

* All recipes serve 4 people.

* All preparation and cooking times are approximate and should be used as a guide only.

* Always pre-heat the oven and cook on the middle shelf unless otherwise stated in a recipe.

* Soya margarine and oil are called for in the recipes. Substitute sunflower or olive varieties if you prefer.

* Dairy products are used throughout this book and some recipes include non–vegetarian cheeses such as Camembert and Stilton. Vegetarian types can be substituted if you prefer. Remember that even cottage and curd cheese contain rennet which is derived from calves.

* Many recipes call for vegetable stock. Substitute 2.5 ml/ $1/2$ tsp yeast extract dissolved in 300 ml/$1/2$ pt/$1 1/4$ cups boiling water instead if you prefer.

* Please note that Worcestershire sauce contains anchovies. Look for the vegetarian alternative in health food shops.

* Many recipes call for dried beans or pulses (see below for cooking hints). Alternatively substitute a 420 g/15 oz can for every 100 g/4 oz/$2/3$ cup dried beans.

* The recipes call for skimmed milk. Use semi-skimmed if you prefer (and whole milk for children under two).

* Most recipes call for wholemeal flour and bread as it has a higher fibre content; however you can substitute white varieties if you prefer.

* Microwave recipes were produced using a 650w oven with revolving turntable.

* *M* means recipe is suitable for microwaving.

* *F* means recipe is suitable for freezing.

* All eggs are size 2 or 3 unless otherwise stated.

* Always wash fresh produce before use and peel if necessary.

As you begin to encourage your family towards a healthier diet, ensure that you use wholemeal produce and the low sugar, low salt, varieties of tinned food. Common sense will tell you to avoid highly processed food and to use fresh produce whenever possible.

# Cooking Pulses

* It's important when cooking all pulses, except red lentils, to soak them for several hours (preferably overnight) beforehand. To speed up this process, use boiling water and leave for two hours.

* When soaked, drain and place in a large saucepan of cold water. Do not add salt as this will toughen skins. Bring the water to the boil and boil rapidly for 10 minutes. This is essential to destroy any toxins in the beans. Then reduce heat and simmer until tender (this can be anything from 1-3 hours depending on the variety). Drain and use as required.

* To save fuel, cook more than you require for a recipe then cool and store remainder in the fridge for several days, or freeze for future use.

# Pastry Making

Few of the recipes in this book call for making pastry, but if you want to make sweet or savoury pies, simply use your normal pastry recipe, but instead of using lard (shortening) and ordinary margarine, use all vegetable margarine or half white vegetable fat (like white Flora) and half vegetable margarine. Use plain (all-purpose) flour or wholemeal (graham) flour, or a mixture of the two.

# CHAPTER 1

# SOUPS AND STARTERS

**S**ome of the soups are filling enough for a light meal. Many of the starters will make nutritious lunch or supper dishes with the addition of a jacket potato or some hot, crusty bread.

Vegetarian food is extremely versatile, so don't be afraid to experiment.

# All-Year Tomato Soup

| *M* *F* Serves 4 | Metric | Imperial | American |
|---|---|---|---|
| Soya margarine | 25 g | 1 oz | 2 tbsp |
| Onion, chopped | 1 | 1 | 1 |
| Stick (rib) celery, finely chopped | 1 | 1 | 1 |
| Can tomatoes | 400 g | 14 oz | 14 oz |
| Wholemeal (graham) flour | 30 ml | 2 tbsp | 2 tbsp |
| Vegetable stock | 600 ml | 1 pt | 2$^{1}/_{2}$ cups |
| Chopped basil | 5 ml | 1 tsp | 1 tsp |
| Salt and pepper | | | |
| Tomato purée (paste) | 20 ml | 4 tsp | 4 tsp |
| Worcestershire sauce | 5 ml | 1 tsp | 1 tsp |
| Skimmed milk | 150 ml | $^{1}/_{4}$ pt | $^{2}/_{3}$ cup |
| Fresh chopped parsley | | | |

1. Melt the margarine in a large pan. Add the onion and fry (sauté) for 3 minutes, stirring.

2. Add the celery and cook for 2 minutes, stirring.

3. Add remaining ingredients and cover. Bring to the boil, reduce heat and simmer for 10 minutes or until vegetables are soft.

4. Cool slightly then liquidise in a food processor or blender or pass through a sieve (strainer). Reheat, taste and re-season if necessary.

5. Ladle into warm soup bowls and sprinkle with chopped parsley before serving.

Preparation time: 5 minutes
Cooking time: 15 minutes

# Cheese and Vegetable Soup

This is a very simple cheese soup, to which all sorts of extra ingredients can be added. For a more sophisticated starter use Stilton instead of Cheddar cheese. Either way, the soup is delicious.

| *M* *F* Serves 4 | Metric | Imperial | American |
|---|---|---|---|
| Soya margarine | 50 g | 2 oz | 1/4 cup |
| Onion, chopped | 1 | 1 | 1 |
| Finely chopped celery | 30 ml | 2 tbsp | 2 tbsp |
| Wholemeal (graham) flour | 25 g | 1 oz | 1/4 cup |
| Made mustard | 5 ml | 1 tsp | 1 tsp |
| Skimmed milk | 600 ml | 1 pt | 2 1/2 cups |
| Vegetable stock | 150 ml | 1/4 pt | 2/3 cup |
| Salt and pepper | | | |
| Vegetarian Cheddar cheese, grated | 100 g | 4 oz | 1 cup |
| Chopped parsley to garnish | | | |
| **Optional extras:** | | | |
| Finely chopped raw mushrooms | 100 g | 4 oz | 2 cups |
| A little cooked sweetcorn, peas etc. | | | |

1. Melt the margarine in a pan. Add the onion and fry (sauté) for 3 minutes, stirring.

2. Add the wholemeal flour and mustard and cook for 1 minute. Gradually blend in the milk and vegetable stock and bring to the boil, stirring.

3. Reduce heat, cover and continue cooking for 10 minutes, stirring occasionally. Season and add the cheese and any other ingredients you wish at this point.

4. Cover and simmer for a further 5 minutes. Pour into warmed bowls and garnish with parsley.

Serve with Celery and Cheese Loaf (see recipe p134).

To turn this into a fun mainmeal for the family, serve each bowl of soup with a side plate containing a selection of crudités to dip and dunk in, eg carrot sticks, celery sticks, tomato quarters, raw mushrooms, cauliflower florets, cheese sticks, chunks of fresh bread, etc.

Preparation time: 3 minutes
Cooking time: 20 minutes

# Chestnut and Carrot Soup

| *M* *F* Serves 4 | Metric | Imperial | American |
|---|---|---|---|
| Soya or sunflower oil | 15 ml | 1 tbsp | 1 tbsp |
| Onion, chopped | 1 | 1 | 1 |
| Chopped carrots | 225 g | 8 oz | 2 cups |
| Can unsweetened chestnut purée | 350 g | 12 oz | 12 oz |
| Vegetable stock | 450 ml | ¾ pt | 2 cups |
| Ground bay leaves (or 1 whole one) | 5 ml | 1 tsp | 1 tsp |
| Can tomatoes | 400 g | 14 oz | 14 oz |
| Tomato purée (paste) | 30 ml | 2 tbsp | 2 tbsp |
| Salt and pepper | | | |
| Worcestershire sauce | 5 ml | 1 tsp | 1 tsp |
| Chopped parsley to garnish | | | |
| To serve: | | | |
| Herby Baps (page 138) | | | |

1. Heat the oil and fry (sauté) the onion and carrot in a large pan for 3 minutes, stirring.

2. Add remaining ingredients, cover and simmer for 10-15 minutes until the vegetables are soft.

3. Remove the bay leaf, if whole, liquidise in a blender or food processor, or pass through a sieve (strainer). Reheat if necessary.

4. Garnish with chopped parsley before serving with Herby Baps.

Preparation time: 5 minutes
Cooking time: 13-18 minutes

# Mushroom Soup

This is a delicious soup but if you halve the quantity of liquid it can also be used as an excellent mushroom sauce to go with pastry dishes or nut roasts, etc.

| *M* *F* Serves 4 | Metric | Imperial | American |
|---|---|---|---|
| *Soya margarine* | *25 g* | *1 oz* | *2 tbsp* |
| *Button mushrooms* | *225 g* | *8 oz* | *4 cups* |
| *Onion, chopped* | *1* | *1* | *1* |
| *Wholemeal (graham) flour* | *15 ml* | *1 tbsp* | *1 tbsp* |
| *Ground mace* | *5 ml* | *1 tsp* | *1 tsp* |
| *Vegetable stock* | *600 ml* | *1 pt* | *2¹/₂ cups* |
| *Skimmed milk* | *150 ml* | *¹/₄ pt* | *²/₃ cup* |
| *Salt and pepper* | | | |
| *Chopped parsley to garnish* | | | |
| *To serve:* | | | |
| *Cheese 'Rolls' (page 147)* | | | |

1. Melt the margarine in a pan and fry (sauté) the onion for 3 minutes stirring.

2. Add the mushrooms and continue cooking for 1 minute, stirring. Add the flour and mace and cook for a further minute.

3. Gradually stir in the stock and milk, bring to the boil stirring. Cover, reduce heat and simmer for 10 minutes, stirring occasionally. Season to taste.

4. Liquidise in a blender or food processor if liked. Reheat and serve in warmed bowls. Add a few sliced raw mushrooms or a spoonful of crème fraiche with the parsley, if liked. Serve with cheese 'Rolls'.

Preparation time: 5 minutes
Cooking time: 15 minutes

# Watercress Soup

Watercress makes a really tasty soup and it is extremely good for you as it is full of iron. The potato thickens the soup without having to use any flour.

| *M* *F* Serves 4 | Metric | Imperial | American |
|---|---|---|---|
| Soya margarine | 25 g | 1 oz | 2 tbsp |
| Bunches of watercress, roughly chopped | 2 | 2 | 2 |
| Medium potato, chopped | 1 | 1 | 1 |
| Medium onion, chopped | 1 | 1 | 1 |
| Celery seeds | 2.5 ml | 1/2 tsp | 1/2 tsp |
| Skimmed milk | 450 ml | 3/4 pt | 2 cups |
| Vegetable stock | 300 ml | 1/2 pt | 1 1/4 cups |
| Salt and pepper | | | |
| To garnish: | | | |
| Crème fraiche | | | |

1. Melt the margarine in a large saucepan. Add the watercress, potato, onion and celery seeds and fry (sauté) gently, stirring, for 5 minutes.

2. Add the milk and stock and season to taste.

3. Bring to the boil, reduce heat and simmer for 10-15 minutes, until the vegetables are soft.

4. Cool slightly then liquidise in a food processor or blender or pass through a sieve (strainer). Reheat.

5. Taste and re-season if necessary. Ladle into bowls. Add a swirl of crème fraiche to garnish.

**Note:**
This recipe is just as delicious made with lettuce instead of watercress. Use when there is a glut of lettuces in the summer.

Preparation time: 10 minutes
Cooking time: 15-20 minutes

# Baked Bean Pâté

This makes a lovely sandwich filling for the children and an unusual starter for adults too!

| *F* Serves 4 | Metric | Imperial | American |
|---|---|---|---|
| Can reduced sugar and salt baked beans | 420 g | 15 oz | 15 oz |
| Vegetarian Cheddar cheese, grated | 100 g | 4 oz | 1 cup |
| Fresh breadcrumbs | 50g | 2 oz | 1 cup |
| Yeast extract | 5 ml | 1 tsp | 1 tsp |
| Dried mixed herbs | 5 ml | 1 tsp | 1 tsp |
| Salt and pepper | | | |
| *To serve:* | | | |
| Fresh vegetables cut into matchsticks or small florets | | | |

1. Place all ingredients in a food processor or blender and process for 1½ minutes.

2. Turn out into a container. Chill until ready to serve with fresh vegetable 'dippers'.

Preparation time: 5 minutes plus chilling

# Blue Cheese Mushrooms

| *M* Serves 4 | Metric | Imperial | American |
|---|---|---|---|
| Large flat mushrooms, peeled | 225 g | 8 oz | 4 cups |
| Soya margarine | 50 g | 2 oz | 1/4 cup |
| Shallots, finely chopped | 2 | 2 | 2 |
| Vegetarian blue cheese, crumbled | 175 g | 6 oz | 1 1/2 cups |
| Fresh breadcrumbs | 25 g | 1 oz | 1/2 cup |
| Salt and pepper | | | |

1. Remove the mushroom stalks and chop.

2. Melt the margarine in a pan, add the stalks and shallots and cook for 2 minutes, stirring.

3. Leave to cool for 5 minutes, then add the cheese and breadcrumbs. Season and mix well. Divide between the mushroom caps.

4. Grease a large shallow dish and place the mushroom caps in it. Add 30 ml/2 tbsp water. Cover with foil and bake for 12 minutes at 200°C/400°F/gas mark 6, until the mushrooms are cooked and topping is bubbling.

**Note:**
If cooking in the microwave do not add water, do not cover dish and cook for 2 minutes on high.

Preparation time: 5 minutes
Cooking time: 15 minutes

# Camembert Tomatoes

You can use vegetarian Cheddar or Cheshire instead if you prefer.

| Serves 4 | Metric | Imperial | American |
|---|---|---|---|
| *Large tomatoes, halved* | *4* | *4* | *4* |
| *Camembert cheese, derinded and chopped* | *225 g* | *8 oz* | *2 cups* |
| *fresh breadcrumbs* | *50 g* | *2 oz* | *1 cup* |
| *A little fresh chopped parsley* | | | |
| ***To serve:*** | | | |
| *Watercress* | | | |

1. Remove seeds from the tomatoes and place the 'shells' on serving plate.

2. Mix the chopped cheese with the breadcrumbs and fill halved tomatoes. Sprinkle with parsley.

3. Place under a moderately hot grill (broiler) for 2 minutes or until cheese melts, taking care that breadcrumbs do not burn. Serve in a ring of watercress.

Preparation time: 5 minutes
Cooking time: 2 minutes

# Cheesy Avocados

Serve as a starter or with a colourful salad and wholemeal bread for lunch.

| *M* Serves 4 | Metric | Imperial | American |
|---|---|---|---|
| Mayonnaise (page 152) | 10 ml | 2 tsp | 2 tsp |
| Tomato purée (paste) | 5 ml | 1 tsp | 1 tsp |
| Tabasco sauce | 2 drops | 2 drops | 2 drops |
| Salt and Pepper | | | |
| Ripe avocados, halved and stoned (pitted) | 4 | 4 | 4 |
| Slices vegetarian Cheddar cheese | 8 | 8 | 8 |
| *To serve:* | | | |
| Garlic bread (page 137) | | | |

1. Mix together the mayonnaise, tomato purée, Tabasco sauce, salt and pepper.

2. Fill cavities in avocados with mixture.

3. Place slices of cheese over the top.

4. Grill (broil) gently, until cheese melts (about 3 minutes).

5. Serve with garlic bread.

Preparation time: 3 minutes
Cooking time: 3 minutes

# Curried Egg Mayonnaise

This makes an ideal sandwich filler or a delicious starter when served on a bed of watercress, or other green salad item.

| Serves 4 | Metric | Imperial | American |
|---|---|---|---|
| *Hard–boiled (hard-cooked) eggs, chopped* | *4* | *4* | *4* |
| *Chutney (see page 153)* | *15 ml* | *1 tbsp* | *1 tbsp* |
| *Mayonnaise (see page 152)* | *45 ml* | *3 tbsp* | *3 tbsp* |
| *Salt and pepper* | | | |
| *Curry powder* | *5 ml* | *1 tsp* | *1 tsp* |

1. Mix all the ingredients together. Chill until ready to serve.

Preparation time: 10 minutes plus chilling

# **Fruity Melon Starter**

If you have a filling main course and dessert, this makes a lovely light beginning to a meal. Vary the fruit according to what's in season.

| Serves 4 | Metric | Imperial | American |
|---|---|---|---|
| *Ripe honeydew melon, quartered, seeded (pitted) and skinned* | *1* | *1* | *1* |
| *Half fat cottage cheese* | *225 g* | *8 oz* | *1 cup* |
| *Skimmed milk* | *15 ml* | *1 tbsp* | *1 tbsp* |
| *Black and green grapes, halved and seeded (pitted)* | *100 g* | *4 oz* | *1 cup* |
| *To garnish:* | | | |
| *Toasted flaked almonds* | | | |

1. Cut the melon into thin slices and arrange attractively on serving plates.

2. Beat cottage cheese and milk together and fold in grapes.

3. Just before serving, spoon over or beside the melon slices.

4. Garnish with a few toasted flaked almonds.

Preparation time: 5 minutes

# Herby Bites

These make a delicious starter when served on a bed of shredded lettuce, or for a special occasion use frisée, dotted with cherry tomatoes.

| Serves 4 | Metric | Imperial | American |
|---|---|---|---|
| *Curd cheese* | *225 g* | *8 oz* | *1 cup* |
| *Dry roasted peanuts, ground (see page 155)* | *60 ml* | *4 tbsp* | *4 tbsp* |
| *Spring onions (scallions), chopped* | *4* | *4* | *4* |
| *Chopped parsley* | *15 ml* | *1 tbsp* | *1 tbsp* |
| *Chopped (snipped) chives* | *15 ml* | *1 tbsp* | *1 tbsp* |
| *Chopped tarragon* | *15 ml* | *1 tbsp* | *1 tbsp* |
| *Salt and pepper* | | | |

1. Mix all the ingredients together thoroughly, reserving 30 ml/2 tbsp ground peanuts.

2. Form into 2.5 cm/1 in balls, roll in the remaining ground peanuts. Chill, before serving.

Preparation time: 10 minutes plus chilling

# Mushroom Cocktail

| Serves 4 | Metric | Imperial | American |
|---|---|---|---|
| Button mushrooms, halved or quartered | 225 g | 8 oz | 4 cups |
| Peanuts, dry roasted (see page 155) | 50 g | 2 oz | ½ cup |
| Mixed black and green grapes, halved and seeded (pitted) | 100 g | 4 oz | 1 cup |
| Cocktail sauce: | | | |
| Mayonnaise | 60 ml | 4 tbsp | 4 tbsp |
| Tomato purée (paste) | 5 ml | 1 tsp | 1 tsp |
| Worcestershire sauce | few drops | few drops | few drops |
| Salt and pepper | | | |
| To garnish: | | | |
| Sunflower seeds | | | |
| To serve: | | | |
| Shredded lettuce | | | |

1. Blanch the mushrooms if preferred or leave raw.

2. Mix with the peanuts and grapes.

3. Blend cocktail sauce ingredients together. Fold in mushroom mixture. Sprinkle with sunflower seeds.

4. Serve on a bed of shredded lettuce.

## Note:

For a special occasion substitute the peanuts with cashew nuts.

Preparation time: 5 minutes

# Potted Cheese

Try using crumbled vegetarian blue cheese and port instead of Cheddar and sherry. This also makes a delicious sandwich filling or savoury end to a dinner party instead of the usual cheese board.

| *F* Serves 4 | Metric | Imperial | American |
|---|---|---|---|
| Soya margarine | 100g | 4 oz | 1/2 cup |
| Ground mace | pinch | pinch | pinch |
| Salt and pepper | | | |
| Grated vegetarian Cheddar cheese | 225 g | 8 oz | 2 cups |
| Skimmed milk | 15 ml | 1 tbsp | 1 tbsp |
| Sherry | 15 ml | 1 tbsp | 1 tbsp |
| To serve: | | | |
| Crackers or crisp toast and sticks of fresh vegetables | | | |

1. Mix all the ingredients together. Pack into one large or four small pots.

2. Cover and chill.

Preparation time: 5 minutes

# Red Devil Pâté

| *F* Serves 4 | Metric | Imperial | American |
|---|---|---|---|
| *Can red kidney beans, drained* | *420 g* | *15 oz* | *15 oz* |
| *Tomato purée* | *15 ml* | *1 tbsp* | *1 tbsp* |
| *Soy sauce* | *5 ml* | *1 tsp* | *1 tsp* |
| *Lemon juice* | *5 ml* | *1 tsp* | *1 tsp* |
| *Few drops of Tabasco sauce* | | | |
| *Salt and pepper* | | | |
| *To garnish:* | | | |
| *Paprika* | | | |
| *To serve:* | | | |
| *Bread or toast, salad* | | | |

1. Put all ingredients into a blender or food processor.

2. Liquidise for 2-3 minutes until mixture is smooth. Moisten with a little vegetable stock if necessary. Turn into a bowl and chill.

3. Garnish with paprika and serve with a salad and hot crusty wholemeal bread for lunch, or just with wholemeal toast or rye bread as a delicious starter.

Preparation time: 5 minutes plus chilling

# Spicy Red Lentil Pâté

| *M* *F* Serves 4 | Metric | Imperial | American |
|---|---|---|---|
| Red lentils | 100 g | 4 oz | 2/3 cup |
| Boiling water | 450 g | 3/4 pt | 2 cups |
| Desiccated (shredded) coconut | 50 g | 2 oz | 1/2 cup |
| Lemon juice | 10 ml | 2 tsp | 2 tsp |
| Tabasco sauce | 4 drops | 4 drops | 4 drops |
| Salt and pepper | | | |
| Ground nutmeg | pinch | pinch | pinch |
| To serve: | | | |
| Tortilla Chips | | | |

1. Put the lentils and water into a large pan. Bring to the boil and reduce heat. Cover and simmer for 12 minutes or until soft.

2. Drain and reserve the liquid.

3. Stir in the coconut, lemon juice, Tabasco sauce, salt, pepper and nutmeg.

4. Put in a food processor or blender and liquidise until smooth, adding a little reserved stock if necessary.

5. Chill thoroughly before serving with Tortilla chips.

Preparation time: 5 minutes plus chilling
Cooking time: 12 minutes

# Tomato and Goat's Cheese Platter

| Serves 4 | Metric | Imperial | American |
|---|---|---|---|
| *Tomatoes, sliced* | 6 | 6 | 6 |
| *Goat's cheese, sliced* | 100 g | 4 oz | 1 cup |
| *Black olives, halved and* | | | |
| *    stoned (pitted)* | 8 | 8 | 8 |
| ***French dressing:*** | | | |
| *Soya oil* | 30 ml | 2 tbsp | 2 tbsp |
| *Vinegar* | 15 ml | 1 tbsp | 1 tbsp |
| *A little mustard powder* | | | |
| *Salt and pepper* | | | |
| ***To garnish:*** | | | |
| *A few chopped (snipped)* | | | |
| *    chives* | | | |

1. Interleaf slices of tomatoes with slices of goat's cheese on individual plates. Sprinkle with the olives.

2. Shake dressing ingredients together in a screw-topped jar.

3. Drizzle over salad and garnish with chopped chives just before serving.

Preparation time: 5 minutes

CHAPTER 2

# MAIN MEALS

**A**ll these recipes are infinitely changeable with a little imagination. Take out, put in, add, or take away according to your family's tastes and what's in the fridge or store cupboard at the time. Cheapness, texture, variety, colour, nutrition, interest and flavour are the key to them all.

# Baked Bean Savoury

| *M* Serves 4 | Metric | Imperial | American |
|---|---|---|---|
| Soya margarine | 25 g | 1 oz | 2 tbsp |
| Onion, chopped | 1 | 1 | 1 |
| Cans low sugar and salt baked beans | 2 × 420 g | 2 × 15 oz | 2 × 15 oz |
| Hard–boiled (hard-cooked) eggs, quartered | 4 | 4 | 4 |
| Salt and pepper | | | |
| Tomato purée (paste) | 5 ml | 1 tsp | 1 tsp |
| Worcestershire sauce | few drops | few drops | few drops |
| Grated vegetarian Cheddar cheese | 100 g | 4 oz | 1 cup |
| Breadcrumbs | 50 g | 2 oz | 1 cup |
| Dried mixed herbs | pinch | pinch | pinch |
| **To serve:** | | | |
| Wholemeal toast, a green salad | | | |

1. Melt the margarine in a pan. Add the onion and fry (sauté) gently, stirring for 5 minutes until soft.

2. Stir in the beans, eggs, a little salt and pepper, the tomato purée and Worcestershire sauce and heat through.

3. Turn into a flameproof casserole (Dutch oven). Mix the cheese and breadcrumbs together and sprinkle over.

4. Place under a hot grill (broiler) until cheese is melted and golden. Serve with toast and a green salad.

Preparation time: 10 minutes
Cooking time: 10 minutes

# 'Busy' Risotto

I call this busy risotto because the essence of its success is that it has to have a lot of different ingredients in it. They can be anything you happen to have left over in the fridge or stored in the cupboard, but give it a good variety of colour and texture to make it interesting. Serve with a large bowl of grated vegetarian Cheddar cheese.

| *M* *F* Serves 4 | Metric | Imperial | American |
|---|---|---|---|
| Onion, chopped | 1 | 1 | 1 |
| Soya margarine | 25 g | 1 oz | 2 tbsp |
| Carrots, chopped | 50 g | 2 oz | 1/2 cup |
| Celery, chopped | 50 g | 2 oz | 1/2 cup |
| Frozen peas | 100 g | 4 oz | 1 cup |
| Mushrooms, sliced | 50 g | 2 oz | 1 cup |
| Brown long grain rice | 225 g | 8 oz | 1 cup |
| Vegetable stock | 600 ml | 1 pt | 2 1/2 cups |
| Worcestershire sauce | 5 ml | 1 tsp | 1 tsp |
| Tomato purée (paste) | 15 ml | 1 tbsp | 1 tbsp |
| Dried mixed herbs | 5 ml | 1 tsp | 1 tsp |
| Salt and pepper | | | |
| Beansprouts | 225 g | 8 oz | 2 cups |
| Dry roasted peanuts (see page 155) | 15 ml | 1 tbsp | 1 tbsp |
| Can sweetcorn (corn) | 200 g | 7 oz | 7 oz |
| Pumpkin seeds | 30 ml | 2 tbsp | 2 tbsp |
| Pulses, cooked, any variety will do | 225 g | 8 oz | 1 1/3 cups |

1. Fry (sauté) the onion in the margarine in a large frying pan (skillet) or wok for 3 minutes stirring.

2. Add the carrots, celery, peas, mushrooms and rice and cook, stirring, for a further 2 minutes.

3. Add the stock, Worcestershire sauce, tomato purée, herbs and seasoning to taste. Bring to the boil.

4. Cover, reduce heat and simmer gently for 30 minutes. Add the beansprouts, peanuts, sweetcorn, seeds and pulses. Re-cover and heat through for 5 minutes. Serve straight from the pan.

Preparation time: 5 minutes
Cooking time: 40 minutes

# Butter Beans and Mushrooms

Ring the changes by using different cooked pulses or a combination of pulses, beans and sweetcorn.

| *M* *F* Serves 4 | Metric | Imperial | American |
|---|---|---|---|
| Soya oil | 30 ml | 2 tbsp | 2 tbsp |
| Mushrooms, sliced | 225 g | 8 oz | 4 cups |
| Plain (all-purpose) or wholemeal flour | 22.5 ml | 1½ tbsp | 1½ tbsp |
| Skimmed milk | 300 ml | ½ pt | 1¼ cups |
| Vegetarian Cheddar cheese, grated | 100 g | 4 oz | 1 cup |
| Butter beans, cooked | 225 g | 8 oz | 1⅓ cups |
| Salt and pepper | | | |
| Grated nutmeg | pinch | pinch | pinch |
| Breadcrumbs | 45 ml | 3 tbsp | 3 tbsp |
| Sesame seeds | 45 ml | 3 tbsp | 3 tbsp |
| Soya margarine | 25 g | 1 oz | 2 tbsp |

1. Heat the oil in a pan. Add the mushrooms and fry (sauté) for 2 minutes, stirring.

2. Add the flour and cook for 1 minute.

3. Stir in the skimmed milk, bring to the boil and cook for 2 minutes, stirring all the time.

4. Add 75 g/3 oz/¾ cup grated cheese, butter beans, seasoning and nutmeg and stir well.

5. Put into a greased ovenproof dish and sprinkle with breadcrumbs, sesame seeds and remainder of grated cheese. Dot with margarine. Bake at 190°C/375°F/gas mark 5 for 30 minutes.

Preparation time: 5 minutes
Cooking time: 35 minutes

# Celery and Cheese Quiche

I often feel that by the time you've gone to the trouble of making pastry you don't always want to spend hours making the rest of the dish. So this recipe is ideal in that the filling is just mixed together and then poured over the pastry case without any pre-cooking. The crunchy celery contrasts well with the rest of the filling. Substitute 320 g/12 oz can of sweetcorn (corn) for the celery, or use left-over cooked vegetables.

| *F* Serves 4 | Metric | Imperial | American |
|---|---|---|---|
| *Pastry case, made with 175 g/ 6 oz /1½ cups wholemeal or plain (all-purpose) flour, baked blind (see page 9)* | *1* | *1* | *1* |
| *Sticks (ribs) of celery, chopped* | *4* | *4* | *4* |
| *Vegetarian Cheddar cheese, sliced thinly* | *100 g* | *4 oz* | *1 cup* |
| *Eggs, any size* | *2* | *2* | *2* |
| *Natural (plain) yoghurt* | *45 ml* | *3 tbsp* | *3 tbsp* |
| *Made mustard* | *5 ml* | *1 tsp* | *1 tsp* |
| *Salt and pepper* | | | |
| *Sesame seeds* | | | |

1. Arrange celery over the bottom of the pastry case and cover with sliced cheese.

2. Beat together eggs, yoghurt, mustard and seasoning. Pour over cheese.

3. Sprinkle with sesame seeds.

4. Bake at 190°C/375°F/gas mark 5 for 35 minutes until filling is set.

Preparation time: 15 minutes
Cooking time: 35 minutes plus baking pastry case

# Cheese Fondue

For our Christmas meal we often like to have something completely different to the traditional fare and occasionally we have a cheese fondue. It is also fun for a children's birthday party.

| *M* Serves 4 | Metric | Imperial | American |
|---|---|---|---|
| *For the fondue:* | | | |
| Dry white wine or dry cider (or milk or apple juice for children) | 300 ml | ½ pt | 1¼ cups |
| Lemon juice | 5 ml | 1 tsp | 1 tsp |
| Grated vegetarian Cheddar cheese | 450 g | 1 lb | 4 cups |
| Cornmeal mixed with 15 ml/ 1 tbsp water | 15 ml | 1 tbsp | 1 tbsp |
| Soya margarine | 25 g | 1 oz | 2 tbsp |
| Salt and pepper | | | |
| Ground nutmeg | pinch | pinch | pinch |

1. Place all the ingredients in a large saucepan or metal fondue pot.

2. Cook gently, stirring all the time until the cheese has melted. Taste and re-season if necessary. Pour into fondue dish and take to the table.

## Things to dip and dunk:

Cubes of bread, cubes of pineapple, halved raw mushrooms, whole baby sweetcorn (corn), quartered tomatoes, carrot and celery chunks, strips of different coloured peppers, water chestnuts, bamboo shoots, savoury biscuits, cauliflower or broccoli florets; the list is endless!

Preparation time: 10 minutes
Cooking time: 6 minutes

# Cheese, Egg and Tagliatelle Ring

I like using the green tagliatelle verdi for this dish, but plain, wholemeal or tomato pasta are also fine to use.

| *M* Serves 4 | Metric | Imperial | American |
|---|---|---|---|
| *Tagliatelle* | *225 g* | *8 oz* | *2 cups* |
| *Vegetarian Cheddar cheese, grated* | *100 g* | *4 oz* | *1 cup* |
| *Fresh chopped parsley* | | | |
| *Can sweetcorn (corn)* | *300 g* | *12 oz* | *12 oz* |
| *White sauce (see page 150)* | *450 ml* | *³/₄ pt* | *2 cups* |
| *Salt and pepper* | | | |
| *Hard–boiled (hard–cooked) eggs, halved* | *8* | *8* | *8* |
| *Paprika* | | | |
| *Grated Parmesan (or vegetarian equivalent) cheese* | | | |

1. Cook the tagliatelle according to packet directions. Drain and keep warm.

2. Add the cheese, parsley and sweetcorn to white sauce and season with salt and pepper. Heat through.

3. Serve the halved eggs in the middle of a ring of tagliatelle topped with sauce and sprinkled with a little paprika and grated Parmesan to garnish.

Preparation time: 10 minutes
Cooking time: 20 minutes

# Cheesy Sweetcorn Grill

This is an extremely versatile and easy to prepare dish. You can replace the beans with six quartered hard–boiled (hard–cooked) eggs, or the sweetcorn with any other cooked chopped vegetable. Also vary the flavour of the white sauce by using herbs, Worcestershire sauce, mustard, peanut butter, etc. Search round the cupboards for an unusual combination.

| *M* *F* Serves 4 | Metric | Imperial | American |
|---|---|---|---|
| Can sweetcorn (corn), drained | 320 g | 12 oz | 12 oz |
| Pulses (any type will do), cooked | 225 g | 8 oz | 1$\frac{1}{3}$ cups |
| White sauce (see page 150) | 450 ml | $\frac{3}{4}$ pt | 2 cups |
| Salt and pepper | | | |
| Grated vegetarian Cheddar cheese | 100 g | 4 oz | 1 cup |
| Nutmeg | pinch | pinch | pinch |
| OR | | | |
| Curry powder | 2.5 ml | 1 tsp | 1 tsp |
| Tabasco sauce | few drops | few drops | few drops |
| To garnish: | | | |
| Paprika | | | |
| To serve: | | | |
| Toast triangles, broccoli | | | |

1. Mix the sweetcorn with the beans or pulses and the white sauce in a saucepan.

2. Add a little salt and pepper, half the cheese and flavourings.

3. Heat through, turn into a flameproof dish and sprinkle with the remaining cheese.

4. Place under a hot grill (broiler) until bubbling and golden brown.

5. Dust with a little paprika. Arrange toast triangles around the edges of the dish and serve with lightly-cooked broccoli.

Preparation: 10-15 minutes
Cooking time: 10-15 minutes

# Chestnut Bake

A can of unsweetened chestnut purée can be very handy to keep in the cupboard not only as the base for a pudding at Christmas time, but for all–year–round savoury dishes as well.

| *M* *F* Serves 4 | Metric | Imperial | American |
|---|---|---|---|
| Onion, chopped | 1 | 1 | 1 |
| Soya oil | 15 ml | 1 tbsp | 1 tbsp |
| Mushrooms, sliced | 225 g | 8 oz | 4 cups |
| Carrots, finely chopped | 100 g | 4 oz | 1 cup |
| Sticks (ribs) of celery , finely chopped | 2 | 2 | 2 |
| Chopped rosemary | 5 ml | 1 tsp | 1 tsp |
| Chopped thyme | 5 ml | 1 tsp | 1 tsp |
| Chopped sage | 5 ml | 1 tsp | 1 tsp |
| Soy sauce | 15 ml | 1 tbsp | 1 tbsp |
| Salt and pepper | | | |
| Can unsweetened chestnut purée | 320 g | 12 oz | 12 oz |
| Vegetable stock | 450 ml | 3/4 pt | 2 cups |
| To serve: | | | |
| Pasta shapes, a mixed salad | | | |

1. Fry (sauté) the onion in the oil for 3 minutes, stirring.

2. Add the mushrooms, carrots and celery and cook for a further 5 minutes, stirring occasionally.

3. Add all seasonings, chestnut purée and stock and mix well. Put into a greased casserole (Dutch oven) and bake at 180°C/350°F/gas mark 4 for 40 minutes. Serve with pasta and a mixed salad.

Preparation time: 5 minutes
Cooking time: 48 minutes

# Chick Pea Goulash

| *M* *F* Serves 4 | Metric | Imperial | American |
|---|---|---|---|
| Soya margarine | 50 g | 2 oz | ¼ cup |
| Garlic clove, crushed | 1 | 1 | 1 |
| Onion, chopped | 1 | 1 | 1 |
| Sliced mushrooms | 100 g | 4 oz | 2 cups |
| Can chopped tomatoes | 400 g | 14 oz | 14 oz |
| Chick peas (garbanzos), cooked | 350 g | 12 oz | 2 cups |
| Tomato purée (paste) | 30 ml | 2 tbsp | 2 tbsp |
| Salt and pepper | | | |
| Paprika | 15 ml | 1 tbsp | |
| Ground cumin | 2.5 ml | ½ tsp | ½ tsp |
| Ground coriander (cilantro) | 2.5 ml | ½ tsp | ½ tsp |
| To garnish: | | | |
| Chopped parsley | | | |
| Soured (dairy sour) cream or natural (plain) yoghurt | | | |
| To serve: | | | |
| Crusty bread, a green salad. | | | |

1. Melt the soya margarine in a pan, add garlic, onion and the mushrooms and fry (sauté) for 3 minutes, stirring.

2. Add all remaining ingredients, cover and simmer gently for 10 minutes. Remove lid and continue cooking for about 5 minutes until the chick peas are bathed in a rich sauce.

3. Spoon into warm bowls. Garnish with chopped parsley and a swirl of soured cream or yoghurt. Serve with crusty bread and a green salad.

Preparation time: 5 minutes
Cooking time: 18 minutes

# Chilli Beans

| *M* *F* Serves 4 | Metric | Imperial | American |
|---|---|---|---|
| Onion, chopped | 1 | 1 | 1 |
| Soya margarine | 50 g | 2 oz | 1/4 cup |
| Wholemeal (graham) flour | 50g | 2 oz | 1/2 cup |
| Chilli (chili) powder | 2.5 ml | 1/2 tsp | 1/2 tsp |
| Ground cumin | 2.5 ml | 1/2 tsp | 1/2 tsp |
| Vegetable stock | 450 ml | 3/4 pt | 2 cups |
| Tomato purée (paste) | 30 ml | 2 tbsp | 2 tbsp |
| Red kidney beans, cooked | 225 g | 8 oz | 2 cups |
| Salt and pepper | | | |
| Chopped oregano | 5 ml | 1 tsp | 1 tsp |
| Chopped parsley | 5 ml | 1 tsp | 1 tsp |
| Pumpkin seeds | 50 g | 2 oz | 2 oz |
| Quark or soured (dairy sour) cream | 30 ml | 2 tbsp | 2 tbsp |
| To serve: | | | |
| Plain rice, shredded lettuce, grated vegetarian Cheddar cheese | | | |

1. Fry (sauté) the onion in the soya margarine for 3 minutes, stirring.

2. Add the flour, chilli powder, and cumin. Continue cooking for 1 minute.

3. Gradually add the stock, bring to the boil and cook for a further 3 minutes, stirring.

4. Add the tomato purée, beans, salt and pepper to taste, the herbs and pumpkin seeds. Cover and simmer gently for 5 minutes.

5. Spoon on to beds of boiled rice, garnish each with a spoonful of quark or soured cream and serve with shredded lettuce and cheese.

Preparation time: 5 minutes
Cooking time: 12 minutes

# Chillied Eggs

A more sophisticated and less bland version of scrambled eggs.

| *M* Serves 4 | Metric | Imperial | American |
|---|---|---|---|
| Soya margarine | 40g | $1^1/_2oz$ | 3 tbsp |
| Onion, chopped | 1 | 1 | 1 |
| Ground ginger | pinch | pinch | pinch |
| Chilli (chili) powder | 1.5 mi | $^1/_4$ tsp | $^1/_4$ tsp |
| Turmeric | 2.5 mi | $^1/_2$ tsp | $^1/_2$ tsp |
| Chopped parsley | 30 mi | 2 tbsp | 2 tbsp |
| Eggs, beaten | 8 | 8 | 8 |
| Salt and pepper | | | |
| Skimmed milk | 100 ml | $3^1/_2$ fl oz | $6^1/_2$ tbsp |
| To serve: | | | |
| Hot toast | | | |

1. Melt the margarine in a saucepan. Add the onion and fry (sauté) for 3 minutes, stirring.

2. Add the spices, parsley, eggs and a little salt and pepper. Whisk in the milk and scramble over a gentle heat. Do not boil.

3. Spoon on to hot toast and serve immediately.

Preparation time: 5 minutes
Cooking time: 6 minutes

# Cottage Cheese Loaf

| Serves 4 | Metric | Imperial | American |
|---|---|---|---|
| Half fat cottage cheese | 225 g | 8 oz | 1 cup |
| Walnuts, chopped | 50 g | 2 oz | 1/2 cup |
| Dried oregano | 2.5 ml | 1/2 tsp | 1/2 tsp |
| Made mustard | 5 ml | 1 tsp | 1 tsp |
| Wholemeal breadcrumbs | 100 g | 4 oz | 2 cups |
| Salt and pepper | | | |
| Eggs, beaten | 2 | 2 | 2 |
| *To serve:* | | | |
| Mixed salad | | | |

1. Mix all the ingredients together well.

2. Turn into a greased 450 g/1 lb loaf tin.

3. Bake in the oven at 180°C/350°F/gas mark 4 for 30 minutes.

4. Leave to cool in the tin for 5 minutes, then turn out and serve cut in slices with a mixed salad.

Preparation time: 3 minutes
Cooking time: 30 minutes

# Country Cottage Pie

This is a good recipe to use to introduce your family to vegetarian food and it's much   tastier than the meaty equivalent.

| *F* Serves 4 | Metric | Imperial | American |
|---|---|---|---|
| Potatoes, cut into small chunks | 450 g | 1 lb | 1 lb |
| Soya margarine | 25 g | 1 oz | 2 tbsp |
| Skimmed milk | 15 ml | 1 tbsp | 1 tbsp |
| Chopped  leftover cooked vegetables (cabbage, swede, carrots, peas, etc.) | 350 g | 12 oz | 3 cups |
| Can reduced sugar and salt baked beans in tomato sauce | 420 g | 15 oz | 15 oz |
| Slices wholemeal bread, chopped | 2 | 2 | 2 |
| Yeast extract | 10 ml | 2 tsp | 2 tsp |
| Boiling water | 30 ml | 2 tbsp | 2 tbsp |
| Salt and pepper | | | |
| Grated vegetarian Cheddar cheese | 75 g | 3 oz | 3/4 cup |
| To serve: | | | |
| A leafy green vegetable | | | |

1. Cook the potatoes in boiling, lightly–salted water until tender.  Drain and mash with the butter and milk.

2. Meanwhile, mix the vegetables with the bread and beans.

3. Dissolve yeast extract in the water and stir into mixture. Season to taste.

4. Turn into an ovenproof dish and cover with the potato. Sprinkle with cheese.

5. Bake at 220°C/420°F/gas mark 7 for 35 minutes or until piping hot and golden brown on top. Serve with a leafy green vegetable.

Preparation time: 20 minutes
Cooking time: 35 minutes

# Crumble Topped Spinach

| *M* *F* Serves 4 | Metric | Imperial | American |
|---|---|---|---|
| Fresh or frozen spinach | 900 g | 2 lb | 2 lb |
| Soya oil | 45 ml | 3 tbsp | 3 tbsp |
| Onion, chopped | 1 | 1 | 1 |
| Salt and pepper | | | |
| Grated nutmeg | 2.5 ml | 1/2 tsp | 1/2 tsp |
| Natural (plain) yoghurt | 150 ml | 1/4 pt | 2/3 cup |
| Wholemeal breadcrumbs | 100 g | 4 oz | 2 cups |
| Chopped nuts, any variety will do | 50 g | 2 oz | 1/2 cup |
| *To serve:* | | | |
| Poached eggs | | | |

1. Wash and drain the spinach, then cook in a covered pan without any extra water for 5 minutes until soft - or according to packet directions, if frozen.

2. Drain well in a colander.

3. Heat 15 ml/1 tbsp of the oil in a pan and fry (sauté) the onion for 3 minutes, stirring.

4. Return spinach to pan, add salt, pepper and nutmeg and continue cooking for 5 minutes, stirring once.

5. Stir in the yoghurt. Put into a greased casserole (Dutch oven). Mix together breadcrumbs, chopped nuts and remainder of oil and sprinkle over the spinach. Bake at 190°C/375°F/gas mark 5 for 20 minutes. Serve hot with poached eggs.

Preparation time: 3 minutes
Cooking time: 28 minutes

# Curried Beans

This sauce is extremely versatile and it makes a good base for any combination of hard–boiled eggs, nuts or vegetables.

| *M* *F* Serves 4 | Metric | Imperial | American |
|---|---|---|---|
| **Sauce:** | | | |
| Soya margarine | 50 g | 2 oz | $^1/_4$ cup |
| Soya oil | 15 ml | 1 tbsp | 1 tbsp |
| Large onion, chopped | 1 | 1 | 1 |
| Wholemeal or plain (all-purpose) flour | 15 ml | 1 tbsp | 1 tbsp |
| Medium hot curry powder | 15 ml | 1 tbsp | 1 tbsp |
| Cloves | 2 | 2 | 2 |
| Tomato purée (paste) | 15 ml | 1 tbsp | 1 tbsp |
| Ground ginger | 1.5 ml | $^1/_4$ tsp | $^1/_4$ tsp |
| Ground cinnamon | 1.5 ml | $^1/_4$ tsp | $^1/_4$ tsp |
| Chutney (see page 153) | 30 ml | 2 tbsp | 2 tbsp |
| Lemon juice | 15 ml | 1 tbsp | 1 tbsp |
| Vegetable stock | 600 ml | 1 pt | $2^1/_2$ cups |
| Salt and pepper | | | |
| Red kidney beans, cooked | 350 g | 12 oz | 3 cups |
| **To garnish:** | | | |
| Desiccated (shredded) coconut, banana, sliced tomato, chutney, nuts. | | | |
| **To serve:** | | | |
| Pat's Perfect Rice (see page 105) and poppadoms | | | |

1. Heat the soya margarine and oil in a large pan. Add the onion and fry (sauté) for 3 minutes, stirring.

2. Add all the remaining ingredients, except beans, stir well, cover, reduce heat and simmer for 25 minutes, stirring occasionally. Add a little more stock if necessary.

3. Add the beans and heat through. Garnish and serve with rice and poppadoms.

### Note:
Poppadoms can be grilled very successfully instead of deep fried to save eating excessive amounts of oil.

Preparation time: 3 minutes
Cooking time: 28 minutes

# Dhal

This is a very quick and easy, but delicious, way of making this old Eastern favourite. It is infinitely versatile – add any cooked vegetables or finely chopped raw vegetables or, alternatively, add cubes of cheese or hard–boiled eggs for more protein. It can be served as a vegetable or the main part of a meal, depending on your other accompaniments.

| *M* *F* Serves 4 | Metric | Imperial | American |
| --- | --- | --- | --- |
| Red lentils | 275 g | 10 oz | good 1¹/₂ cups |
| Vegetable stock | 600 ml | 1 pt | 2¹/₂ cups |
| Bay leaf | 1 | 1 | |
| Salt and pepper | | | |
| Soya margarine | 25 g | 1 oz | 2 tbsp |
| Soya oil | 15 ml | 1 tbsp | 1 tbsp |
| Onion, chopped | 1 | 1 | 1 |
| Ground ginger | 2.5 ml | ¹/₂ tsp | ¹/₂ tsp |
| Ground coriander (cilantro) | 2.5 ml | ¹/₂ tsp | ¹/₂ tsp |
| Ground cumin | 2.5 ml | ¹/₂ tsp | ¹/₂ tsp |

1. Place all the ingredients in a large pan.

2. Bring to the boil, reduce heat, cover and simmer gently for 20 minutes or until the lentils are soft and have absorbed all the liquid. Stir from time to time to prevent sticking.

3. Serve hot.

Preparation time: 2 minutes
Cooking time: 20 minutes

# Lentil Lasagne

Using pre-cooked lasagne cuts down on some of the preparation time in this popular dish, but make sure the sauces are quite runny to compensate, otherwise you will end up with a rather dry dish. This dish is really a meal in itself but stretch it out by serving with a colourful mixed salad and hot crusty wholemeal rolls.

| *M* *F* Serves 4 | Metric | Imperial | American |
|---|---|---|---|
| Red lentils | 225 g | 8 oz | 1¹/₃ cups |
| Boiling water | 900 ml | 1¹/₂ pts | 3³/₄ cups |
| Can chopped tomatoes | 400 g | 14 oz | 14 oz |
| Tomato purée (paste) | 30 ml | 2 tbsp | 2 tbsp |
| Soy sauce | 30 ml | 2 tbsp | 2 tbsp |
| Fresh chopped thyme | 5 ml | 1 tsp | 1 tsp |
| Fresh chopped marjoram | 10 ml | 2 tsp | 2 tsp |
| Salt and pepper | | | |
| Soya oil | 30 ml | 2 tbsp | 2 tbsp |
| Onion, chopped | 1 | 1 | 1 |
| Garlic clove, crushed | 1 | 1 | 1 |
| Carrots, chopped | 100 g | 4 oz | 1 cup |
| Celery, chopped | 100 g | 4 oz | 1 cup |
| Frozen peas | 100 g | 4 oz | 1 cup |
| White sauce (see page 150) | 450 ml | ³/₄ pt | 2 cups |
| Grated nutmeg | 5 ml | 1 tsp | 1 tsp |
| Grated Parmesan | 15 ml | 1 tbsp | 1 tbsp |
| Sheets lasagne | 10 | 10 | 10 |
| Vegetarian Cheddar cheese, grated | 100 g | 4 oz | 1 cup |
| Sesame seeds | | | |
| To garnish: | | | |
| Chopped parsley | | | |

1. Put the lentils in a large pan and pour boiling water over. Bring to the boil, reduce heat, cover and simmer for 15 minutes until just soft.

2. Drain if necessary and add the tomatoes, tomato purée, soy sauce, herbs and seasoning.

3. Heat the oil and fry (sauté) the onion for 3 minutes, stirring. Add the carrots, celery and peas and cook for 15 minutes. Stir in the lentils. Flavour the white sauce with nutmeg and Parmesan cheese.

4. Pour a little white sauce into a large greased shallow dish. Layer lasagne, lentil mixture and white sauce, starting with lasagne and ending with white sauce. Sprinkle with grated cheese and sesame seeds and bake at 190°C/375°F/gas mark 5 for 40 minutes. Garnish with chopped parsley and serve hot.

Preparation time: 10 minutes
Cooking time: 1 hour 10 minutes

# Lentil Supper

This is very tasty and is particularly popular with children.

| *M* *F* Serves 4 | Metric | Imperial | American |
|---|---|---|---|
| Red lentils | 350 g | 12 oz | 2 cups |
| Onion, chopped | 1 | 1 | 1 |
| Vegetable stock | 900 ml | 1½ pts | 3¾ cups |
| Dried mixed herbs | 2.5 ml | ½ tsp | ½ tsp |
| Salt and pepper | | | |
| Wholemeal breadcrumbs | 15 g | ½ oz | ¼ cup |
| Grated vegetarian Cheddar cheese | 75 g | 3 oz | ¾ cup |
| To garnish: | | | |
| Chopped (snipped) chives | | | |
| To serve: | | | |
| Tortilla chips or savoury cracker biscuits | | | |

1. Put the lentils, onion and stock in a large pan. Bring to the boil, reduce heat, cover and simmer gently, stirring occasionally, for about 15 minutes, or until the lentils are cooked and have absorbed all the liquid.

2. Add all the remaining ingredients and reheat for 3 minutes stirring.

3. Spoon into small bowls, garnish with chopped chives and serve with tortilla chips or crackers to dip in.

Preparation time: 5 minutes
Cooking time: 18 minutes

# Melting Marrow

There is often a glut of marrows at the end of the summer and it is difficult to find a sufficient number of interesting recipes to make the most of them. Here are a couple of favourite family recipes.

| *M* Serves 4 | Metric | Imperial | American |
|---|---|---|---|
| Marrow (squash), peeled, seeded and cut into 2.5 cm/1 in pieces | 900 g | 2 lb | 2 lb |
| Soya oil | 30 ml | 2 tbsp | 2 tbsp |
| Soya margarine | 50 g | 2 oz | 1/4 cup |
| Ground coriander (cilantro) | 2.5 ml | 1/2 tsp | 1/2 tsp |
| Ground cumin | 2.5 ml | 1/2 tsp | 1/2 tsp |
| Dried sage | 2.5 ml | 1/2 tsp | 1/2 tsp |
| Salt and pepper | | | |
| Grated vegetarian Cheddar cheese | 175 g | 6 oz | 1 1/2 cups |
| To garnish: | | | |
| Chopped parsley | | | |

1. Put all ingredients except the cheese in a large pan and cook gently, stirring occasionally, for 15 minutes until the marrow is cooked.

2. Remove from heat and stir in the cheese. A lovely sauce is formed by the cheese and marrow juices and should be served over the top of the dish.

3. Serve the marrow with all the cheesy juice spooned over.

Preparation time: 5 minutes
Cooking time: 15 minutes

# Mixed Bean and Cheese Scramble

| *M* Serves 4 | Metric | Imperial | American |
|---|---|---|---|
| Mixed beans or pulses, cooked | 225 g | 8 oz | 1⅓ cups |
| Soya margarine | 50 g | 2 oz | ¼ cups |
| Eggs, beaten | 2 | 2 | 2 |
| Grated vegetarian Cheddar cheese | 100 g | 4 oz | 1 cup |
| Salt and pepper | | | |
| Pinch of cayenne pepper | | | |
| Skimmed milk | 60 ml | 4 tbsp | 4 tbsp |
| Chopped parsley | 45 ml | 3 tbsp | 3 tbsp |
| *To serve:* | | | |
| Hot toast | | | |

1. Put all the ingredients, except parsley, into a large saucepan, mix well and cook gently, stirring until scrambled.

2. Pile on to hot toast and sprinkle with chopped parsley before serving.

Preparation time: 5 minutes
Cooking time: 5 minutes

# Mixed Nut Moussaka

The wine gives a delicious flavour to this dish. But if you prefer, you may use vegetable stock instead.

| *F* Serves 4 | Metric | Imperial | American |
|---|---|---|---|
| *Aubergines (eggplants), sliced* | *2* | *2* | *2* |
| *Salt* | | | |
| *Slices wholemeal (graham) bread, cubed* | *4* | *4* | *4* |
| *Garlic clove, crushed* | *1* | *1* | *1* |
| *Red wine* | *75 ml* | *5 tbsp* | *5 tbsp* |
| *Soya margarine, melted* | *50 g* | *2 oz* | *¼ cup* |
| *Dried oregano* | *5 ml* | *1 tsp* | *1 tsp* |
| *Tomato purée (paste)* | *30 ml* | *2 tbsp* | *2 tbsp* |
| *Water* | *75 ml* | *5 tbsp* | *5 tbsp* |
| *Chopped mixed nuts* | *225 g* | *8 oz* | *2 cups* |
| *Pepper* | | | |
| *Grated vegetarian Cheddar cheese* | *175 g* | *6 oz* | *1½ cups* |
| *White sauce (see page 150)* | *450 ml* | *¾ pt* | *2 cups* |
| *To serve:* | | | |
| *Crusty bread and a mixed salad* | | | |

1. Cook aubergines in boiling, salted water until tender. Drain, rinse with cold water and drain again.

2. Put bread in a bowl with the garlic, wine, melted margarine and the oregano. Mix well.

3. Blend tomato purée with the water and stir in with a fork. Stir in the nuts. Season with a little salt and pepper.

4. Put a layer of about a third of the aubergines in the base of a greased 1.5 litre/2½ pt ovenproof dish.

5. Cover with half the nut mixture. Repeat layers and finish with a final layer of aubergines.

6. Stir half the cheese into white sauce. Spoon over aubergines and sprinkle with remaining cheese.

7. Bake at 200°C/400°F/gas mark 6 for 35 minutes until hot through and top is golden brown. Serve hot with crusty bread and a mixed salad.

Preparation time: 15 minutes
Cooking time: 40 minutes

# North-of-the-Border Marrow

This is quite a substantial dish so serve with something light, like poached eggs or omelettes.

| *M* Serves 4 | Metric | Imperial | American |
|---|---|---|---|
| Marrow (squash), peeled, seeded and cut into 2.5 cm/1 in pieces | 750 g | 1½ lb | 1½ lb |
| Can tomatoes | 400 g | 14 oz | 14 oz |
| Rolled oats | 75 g | 3 oz | scant cup |
| Onion, finely chopped (or chives if you prefer) | 1 | 1 | 1 |
| Fresh chopped mint (or 2.5 ml/ ½ tsp dried) | 5 ml | 1 tsp | 1 tsp |
| Grated vegetarian Cheddar cheese | 175 g | 6 oz | 1½ cups |
| Salt and pepper | | | |
| **To garnish:** | | | |
| Chopped (snipped) chives or parsley | | | |

1. Place all ingredients, except the cheese, in a large pan and simmer, stirring occasionally, for 15-20 minutes, or until the marrow is tender.

2. Stir in grated cheese until melted. Turn into a serving dish and garnish with chives or parsley.

Preparation time: 5 minutes
Cooking time: 15-20 minutes

# Nut Roast Plait

A most impressive and delicious main course meal, special enough to have on the Christmas dinner table. Serve with a mushroom sauce flavoured with a little sherry and traditional Christmas vegetables

| *M* *F* Serves 4 | Metric | Imperial | American |
|---|---|---|---|
| *Chopped mushrooms* | *100 g* | *4 oz* | *2 cup* |
| *Soya margarine* | *50 g* | *2 oz* | *¹/₄ cup* |
| *Quantity Potted Cheese* | | | |
| *(see page 25)* | *1* | *1* | *1* |
| *Simple Bean and Nut Roast* | | | |
| *(see page 72)* | *1* | *1* | *1* |
| *Frozen puff pastry, thawed* | *225 g* | *8 oz* | *8 oz* |
| *Beaten egg to glaze* | *1* | *1* | *1* |
| ***To garnish:*** | | | |
| *Parsley sprigs* | | | |

1. Cook the mushrooms in the margarine for 2 minutes until softened. Leave to cool.

2. Mix in with the Potted Cheese and spread over the top of the Nut Roast.

3. Roll out the pastry into a large rectangle and brush all over with beaten egg.

4. Place the Nut Roast in the centre.

5. Cut the pastry diagonally from within 2.5 cm/1 in of the loaf to outer edge along both sides. Fold ends up over loaf.

6. Plait one strip at a time up and over the top of the loaf, tucking the ends in neatly. Brush with remaining beaten egg.

7. Cook in the oven at 200°C/400°F/gas mark 6 for about 40 minutes, covering with foil half-way through to prevent the pastry over-browning.  Transfer to a serving plate.

8. Garnish with sprigs of parsley and serve hot, cut in slices.

Preparation time: 20 minutes excluding making the Nut Roast
Cooking time: 40 minutes

# One Pot Pasta

This is very handy for making in advance and popping in the freezer in case of emergencies, or to take on a self–catering holiday where cooking facilities are limited, as it is a complete meal in one dish.

| *M* *F* Serves 4 | Metric | Imperial | American |
|---|---|---|---|
| Ribbon noodles | 225 g | 8 oz | 2 cups |
| Can chopped tomatoes | 400 g | 14 oz | 14 oz |
| Grated vegetarian Cheddar | | | |
|    cheese | 100 g | 4 oz | 1 cup |
|    Or | | | |
|    Parmesan cheese, grated | 10 ml | 2 tsp | 2 tsp |
| White sauce (see page 150) | 600 ml | 1 pt | 2¹/₂ cups |
| Hard-boiled (hard-cooked) | | | |
|    eggs | 8 | 8 | 8 |
|    Or | | | |
|    Mixed pulses, cooked | 225 g | 8 oz | 1¹/₃ cups |
| Can sweetcorn (corn) | 320 g | 12 oz | 12 oz |
| Worcestershire sauce | 5 ml | 1 tsp | 1 tsp |
| Salt and pepper | | | |
| Chopped parsley | | | |
| Reduced fat or Hedgehog | | | |
|    crisps (potato chips), | | | |
|    lightly crushed | 3 pkts | 3 pkts | 3 pkts |
| To serve: | | | |
| A green salad | | | |

1. Cook the noodles according to packet directions, drain.

2. Line the base of a large flat greased dish with the tomatoes. Cover with the drained noodles.

3. Add the cheese to the white sauce with the eggs or pulses, sweetcorn, Worcestershire sauce, salt and pepper and parsley and pour over tomatoes and noodles. Freeze now if desired.

4. Cook at 200°C/400°F/gas mark 6 for 40 minutes until well heated through and sprinkle the crisps over the top for the last 5 minutes. Serve with a green salad.

Preparation time: 5 minutes
Cooking time: 50 minutes

# Oriental Rice with Beansprouts

Beansprouts must be one of the most versatile vegetables. With very little preparation – just blanch for 1 minute, if liked, or simply use raw – they can be quickly added to virtually any dish to stretch it out and give it an interesting crunchy texture.

| *M* Serves 4 | Metric | Imperial | American |
|---|---|---|---|
| Soya margarine | 75 g | 3 oz | 1/3 cup |
| Garlic clove, crushed | 1 | 1 | 1 |
| Onion, chopped | 1 | 1 | 1 |
| Sticks (ribs) celery, chopped | 2 | 2 | 2 |
| Green (bell) pepper, chopped | 1 | 1 | 1 |
| Brown long grain rice | 225 g | 8 oz | 1 cup |
| Vegetable stock | 450 ml | 3/4 pt | 2 cups |
| Turmeric | 5 ml | 1 tsp | 1 tsp |
| Ground ginger | 2.5 ml | 1/2 tsp | 1/2 tsp |
| Salt and pepper | | | |
| Mixed pulses, cooked | 100 g | 4 oz | 2/3 cup |
| Can pineapple chunks, drained | 225 g | 8 oz | 8 oz |
| Fresh beansprouts | 350 g | 12 oz | 3 cups |
| To serve: | | | |
| Soy sauce | | | |
| A green salad | | | |

1. Melt 50 g/2 oz/¼ cup of the soya margarine in a large pan. Add the garlic, onion, celery and pepper and fry (sauté) for 2 minutes, stirring.

2. Add the rice, stock, turmeric, ginger and seasoning. Bring to the boil, reduce heat, cover and simmer gently for 25 minutes or until rice is just tender and has absorbed all the stock.

3. Add the pulses, pineapple, beansprouts and remaining soya margarine and heat through, stirring, for a further 3 minutes.

4. Pile on to warm plates and serve with soy sauce and a green salad.

Preparation time: 5 minutes
Cooking time: 30 minutes

# Potato Bake

| *M* Serves 4 | Metric | Imperial | American |
|---|---|---|---|
| *Potatoes, thinly sliced* | *750 g* | *1¹/₂ lb* | *1¹/₂ lb* |
| *Large onion, chopped* | *1* | *1* | *1* |
| *Grated vegetarian Cheddar cheese* | *175 g* | *6 oz* | *1¹/₂ cups* |
| *Chopped thyme* | *5 ml* | *1 tsp* | *1 tsp* |
| *Chopped sage* | *5 ml* | *1 tsp* | *1 tsp* |
| *Salt and pepper* | | | |
| *Grated nutmeg* | *1.5 ml* | *¹/₄ tsp* | *¹/₄ tsp* |
| *Skimmed milk* | *150 ml* | *¹/₄ pt* | *²/₃ cup* |
| *To serve:* | | | |
| *Tomato, Onion and Chive Salad (see page 108)* | | | |

1. Layer the potatoes, onion, cheese, herbs and seasonings into a greased dish and pour over the milk.

2. Cover and cook in the oven at 190°C/375°F/gas mark 5 for 45 minutes to 1 hour or until potatoes are cooked through. Remove cover after 30 minutes to allow top to brown. Serve with Tomato, Onion and Chive salad.

Preparation time: 10 minutes
Cooking time: 45 minutes - 1 hour

# Potato and Cabbage Casserole

| *M* *F* Serves 4 | Metric | Imperial | American |
|---|---|---|---|
| Potatoes, peeled and cut into chunks | 750 g | 1½ lbs | 1½ lbs |
| A little skimmed milk | | | |
| A knob of soya margarine | | | |
| Green cabbage, shredded | 450 g | 1 lb | 4 cups |
| Small onion, peeled and finely chopped – alternatively use chopped (snipped) chives if you find the onion too strong | 1 | 1 | 1 |
| Salt and pepper | | | |
| Grated vegetarian Cheddar cheese | 75 g | 3 oz | ¾ cup |
| Sunflower seeds | | | |
| To serve: | | | |
| Mixed Bean Salad (see page 103) | | | |

1. Cook the potatoes in boiling salted water until just tender. Drain, then mash with a little milk and soya margarine.

2. Cook the cabbage in a little boiling salted water until just tender. Drain.

3. Combine cabbage, onion (or chives), potatoes and seasoning. Put into a greased casserole dish (Dutch oven).

4. Sprinkle grated cheese and sunflower seeds on top and cook at 200°C/400°F/gas mark 6 for 30 minutes until browned. Serve hot with a mixed bean salad.

Preparation time: 5 minutes
Cooking time: 40 minutes

# Red Kidney Bean Croustade

This is the dish that will convert even the most hardened anti-vegetarians. It is very easy to make but looks impressive and is absolutely delicious. Vary the filling ingredients to suit your personal taste.

| *M* *F* Serves 4 | Metric | Imperial | American |
|---|---|---|---|
| **Base:** | | | |
| Mixed chopped nuts | 100 g | 4 oz | 1 cup |
| Grated vegetarian Cheddar cheese | 100 g | 4 oz | 1 cup |
| Slices wholemeal bread | 6 | 6 | 6 |
| Chopped mixed herbs | 5 ml | 1 tsp | 1 tsp |
| Soya oil | 45 ml | 3 tbsp | 3 tbsp |
| **Filling:** | | | |
| Onion, chopped | 1 | 1 | 1 |
| Wholemeal (graham) flour | 30 g | 2 tbsp | 2 tbsp |
| Chilli (chili) powder | 1.5 ml | $1/4$ tsp | $1/4$ tsp |
| Vegetable stock | 300 ml | $1/2$ pt | $1 1/4$ cups |
| Red kidney beans, cooked | 225 g | 8 oz | 2 cups |
| Sunflower seeds | 30 ml | 2 tbsp | 2 tbsp |
| Chopped parsley | | | |
| Salt and pepper | | | |

1. Put all nuts, cheese, bread and herbs into a food processor and process for 1 minute.

2. Add 30 ml/2 tbsp of the soya oil and continue to process for a further minute.

3. Turn into a greased 20 cm/8 in flan dish and press down well. Cook at 190°C/375°F/gas mark 5 for 15 minutes.

4. Meanwhile, make the filling. Fry (sauté) the onion in remaining oil for 2 minutes, stirring.

5. Add the flour and chilli powder and cook for 1 minute.

6. Stir in the stock, bring to the boil and cook for 2 minutes, stirring all the time.

7. Add the red kidney beans, sunflower seeds and parsley, stir well and season to taste.

8. Pour filling over the croustade base and cook in the oven for a further 15 minutes. Serve hot.

Preparation time: 10 minutes
Cooking time: 30 minutes

# Root Vegetable Satay

Use one of the wholefood varieties of peanut butter for this recipe: they are high in fibre and contain no sugar.

| Serves 4 | Metric | Imperial | American |
| --- | --- | --- | --- |
| *Large turnip, cut in bite-sized pieces* | *1* | *1* | *1* |
| *Large carrots, cut in bite-sized pieces* | *2* | *2* | *2* |
| *Large parsnips, cut in bite-sized pieces* | *1* | *1* | *1* |
| *Soya margarine* | *15 ml* | *1 tbsp* | *1 tbsp* |
| *Clear honey* | *15 ml* | *1 tbsp* | *1 tbsp* |
| *Salt and pepper* | | | |
| *Crunchy peanut butter* | *75 ml* | *5 tbsp* | *5 tbsp* |
| *Skimmed milk* | *150 ml* | *1/4 pt* | *2/3 cup* |
| *Chilli (chili) powder* | *1.5 ml* | *1/4 tsp* | *1/4 tsp* |
| *Mixed chopped nuts* | *50 g* | *2 oz* | *1/2 cup* |

1. Cook the vegetables in boiling slightly salted water until just tender. Drain.

2. When cool enough to handle, thread on small wooden skewers.

3. Melt the margarine and honey together. Lay skewers on foil on a grill (broiler) rack.

4. Brush with the margarine and honey and season.

5. Grill (broil), turning occasionally, and brush with the margarine and honey until lightly golden.

6. Meanwhile, warm the milk and peanut butter together in a small pan with the chilli powder, stirring. Pour into 4 small bowls and sprinkle with nuts.

7. Arrange vegetable skewers on warm serving plates with the bowls of sauce. Serve hot.

Preparation time: 20 minutes
Cooking time: 20 minutes

# Savoury Golden Pudding

| *M* Serves 4 | Metric | Imperial | American |
|---|---|---|---|
| Can sweetcorn (corn), drained | 320 g | 12 oz | 12 oz |
| Skimmed milk | 450 ml | ³/₄ pt | 2 cups |
| Eggs, beaten | 3 | 3 | 3 |
| Chopped (snipped) chives | 30 ml | 2 tbsp | 2 tbsp |
| Soya margarine | 25 g | 1 oz | 2 tbsp |
| Salt and pepper | | | |
| Made mustard | 5 ml | 1 tsp | 1 tsp |
| Grated vegetarian Cheddar cheese | 50 g | 2 oz | ¹/₂ cup |
| *To garnish:* | | | |
| Chopped parsley | | | |
| *To serve:* | | | |
| Crusty bread and a mixed salad | | | |

1. Mix all the ingredients together and place in a greased ovenproof dish.

2. Bake at 190°C/375°F/gas mark 5 for about 25-30 minutes until set and golden on top.

3. Sprinkle with chopped parsley and serve with crusty bread and a mixed salad.

Preparation time: 3 minutes
Cooking time: 25-30 minutes

# Savoury Sandwich Bake

This can be prepared in advance, covered then cooked later. Spread margarine thinly to keep the fat content down. Serve with a salad.

| *M* *F* Serves 4 | Metric | Imperial | American |
|---|---|---|---|
| *Slices bread, spread with a little soya margarine* | 6 | 6 | 6 |
| *Yeast extract* | | | |
| *Sliced vegetarian Cheddar cheese* | *100 g* | *4 oz* | *1 cup* |
| *Tomatoes, sliced* | *3* | *3* | *3* |
| *Eggs* | *3* | *3* | *3* |
| *Skimmed milk* | *300 ml* | *½ pt* | *1¼ cups* |
| *Salt and pepper* | | | |
| *Cayenne pepper* | *pinch* | *pinch* | *pinch* |
| *Sesame seeds* | | | |
| *To garnish:* | | | |
| *Chopped parsley* | | | |
| *To serve:* | | | |
| *Coleslaw (see page 96) or a green salad* | | | |

1. Make up sandwiches using bread and margarine, yeast extract, cheese and tomatoes and cut into four.

2. Place in the base of a flat, greased baking dish (pan).

3. Beat together eggs, milk, salt, pepper and cayenne pepper and pour over sandwiches. Sprinkle with sesame seeds.

4. Bake in oven at 190°C/375°F/gas mark 5 for about 40 minutes until set and golden brown. Garnish with chopped parsley and serve with coleslaw or a green salad.

Preparation time: 10 minutes
Cooking time: 40 minutes

# Simple Bean and Nut Roast

This recipe is infinitely versatile: omit nuts and add some finely chopped cooked vegetables, or use cooked lentils instead of pulses.

| *M* *F* Serves 4 | Metric | Imperial | American |
|---|---|---|---|
| Soya oil | 30 ml | 2 tbsp | 2 tbsp |
| Onion, chopped | 1 | 1 | 1 |
| Pulses, any variety will do, cooked | 225 g | 8 oz | 1¹/₃ cups |
| Mixed chopped nuts | 100 g | 4 oz | 1 cup |
| Grated vegetarian Cheddar cheese | 100 g | 4 oz | 1 cup |
| Eggs, beaten | 2 | 2 | 2 |
| Yeast extract | 5 ml | 1 tsp | 1 tsp |
| Chopped marjoram | 2.5 ml | ¹/₂ tsp | ¹/₂ tsp |
| Chopped sage | 2.5 ml | ¹/₂ tsp | ¹/₂ tsp |
| Salt and pepper | | | |
| *To serve:* | | | |
| Broccoli in Tomato Sauce (see page 92) | | | |

1. Heat the oil and fry (sauté) the onion for 3 minutes, stirring.

2. Mash the pulses and mix well with remaining ingredients and onion.

3. Place mixture in a greased 450 g/1 lb loaf tin and bake at 190°C/375°F/gas mark 5 for 30 minutes or until set. Leave to cool slightly, then turn out and serve with Broccoli in Tomato Sauce. Serve with a sauce or juicy vegetables.

Preparation time: 5 minutes
Cooking time: 33 minutes

# Soya Bean Roast

| *F* Serves 4 | Metric | Imperial | American |
|---|---|---|---|
| Dried breadcrumbs | 15 ml | 1 tbsp | 1 tbsp |
| Soya beans, cooked | 100 g | 4 oz | 2/3 cup |
| Leek, sliced | 1 | 1 | 1 |
| Small parsnip, grated | 1 | 1 | 1 |
| Small potato, grated | 1 | 1 | 1 |
| Carrot, grated | 1 | 1 | 1 |
| Soya margarine | 25 g | 1 oz | 2 tbsp |
| Curry paste | 15 ml | 1 tbsp | 1 tbsp |
| Wholemeal (graham) breadcrumbs | 25 g | 1 oz | 1/2 cup |
| Mango chutney (or chutney recipe page 153) | 15 ml | 1 tbsp | 1 tbsp |
| Salt and pepper | | | |
| Egg, beaten | 1 | 1 | 1 |
| **Sauce:** | | | |
| Cucumber, finely chopped | 1/4 | | 1/4 |
| Garlic clove, crushed | 1 | 1 | 1 |
| Dried mint | 10 ml | 2 tsp | 2 tsp |
| Natural (plain) yoghurt | 300 ml | 1/2 pt | 1 1/4 cups |
| **To serve:** | | | |
| Curried cabbage (see page 100) | | | |

1. Grease a 450 g/1lb loaf tin and sprinkle with the dried breadcrumbs.

2. Mash the soya beans well.

3. Fry (sauté) the leek, parsnip, potato and carrot in the soya margarine, stirring for 1 minute. Cover and cook gently for 10 minutes, stirring occasionally.

4. Stir in the curry paste, breadcrumbs, mango chutney and the soya beans. Mix together and season well. Stir in the beaten egg.

5. Turn into prepared tin, cover with foil and bake at 190°C/375°F/gas mark 5 for 1½ hours or until firm.

6. Meanwhile, make the sauce. Mix the cucumber, garlic, mint and yoghurt together in a bowl and season lightly.

7. Leave roast to cool slightly for 10 minutes, then turn out and serve sliced with the sauce and curried cabbage.

Preparation time: 15 minutes
Cooking time: 1¾ hours

# Spaghetti with Lentils, Tomatoes and Herbs

Add chopped vegetables, such as red or green peppers, celery or sweetcorn, to make this dish even more nutritious.

| *M* *F* Serves 4 | Metric | Imperial | American |
|---|---|---|---|
| *Green lentils* | *225 g* | *8 oz* | *1¹/₃ cups* |
| *Can tomatoes* | *400 g* | *14 oz* | *14 oz* |
| *Vegetable stock* | *400 ml* | *1 pt* | *2¹/₂ cups* |
| *Onion, chopped* | *1* | *1* | *1* |
| *Fresh chopped oregano* | *15 ml* | *1 tbsp* | *1 tbsp* |
| *Fresh chopped marjoram* | *15 ml* | *1 tbsp* | *1 tbsp* |
| *Fresh chopped basil* | *15 ml* | *1 tbsp* | *1 tbsp* |
| *Fresh chopped parsley* | *15 ml* | *1 tbsp* | *1 tbsp* |
| *Spaghetti* | *225 g* | *8 oz* | *2 cups* |
| *To serve:* | | | |
| *Grated vegetarian Cheddar or Parmesan cheese* | | | |

1. Put all the ingredients except the spaghetti into a large bowl early in the day. Cover and leave for a few hours.

2. Transfer to a saucepan. Bring to the boil, reduce heat, cover and simmer for about 30 minutes or until the lentils are soft.

3. Meanwhile, cook the spaghetti according to packet directions. Drain.

4. Divide spaghetti between four serving plates. Spoon sauce over and serve with grated cheese.

Preparation time: 5 minutes plus soaking
Cooking time: 30 minutes

# Spaghetti with Piquant Bean Sauce

| *M* *F* Serves 4 | Metric | Imperial | American |
|---|---|---|---|
| Spaghetti | 350 g | 12 oz | 3 cups |
| Soya oil | 30 ml | 2 tbsp | 2 tbsp |
| Garlic clove, crushed | 1 | 1 | 1 |
| Onion, chopped | 1 | 1 | 1 |
| Curry powder | 15 ml | 1 tbsp | 1 tbsp |
| Wholenut peanut butter | 45 ml | 3 tbsp | 3 tbsp |
| Tomato purée | 10 ml | 2 tsp | 2 tsp |
| Lemon juice | 5 ml | 1 tsp | 1 tsp |
| Vegetable stock | 300 ml | 1/2 pt | 1 1/4 cups |
| Salt and pepper | | | |
| Haricot (navy) beans, cooked | 225 g | 8 oz | 1 1/3 cups |
| To serve: | | | |
| Watercress, Orange and Onion Salad (see page 109) | | | |

1. Cook the spaghetti according to packet directions. Drain.

2. Meanwhile, fry (sauté) the garlic and onion in the oil in a pan for 3 minutes, stirring.

3. Add remaining ingredients, cover and simmer for 7 minutes, stirring occasionally.

4. Add to spaghetti and toss well.

5. Serve hot with Watercress, Orange and Onion Salad.

Preparation time: 15 minutes, including cooking spaghetti
Cooking time: 8 minutes

# Spaghetti Volognaise

| *M* *F* Serves 4 | Metric | Imperial | American |
|---|---|---|---|
| *Sauce:* | | | |
| *Haricot (navy), borlotti, red kidney or cannellini beans, cooked* | 225 g | 8 oz | 2 cups |
| *Soya or olive oil* | 15 ml | 1 tbsp | 1 tbsp |
| *Garlic clove, crushed* | 1 | 1 | 1 |
| *Onion, chopped* | 1 | 1 | 1 |
| *Sticks (ribs) celery, washed and chopped* | 3 | 3 | 3 |
| *Carrots, chopped* | 4 | 4 | 4 |
| *Wholemeal (graham) flour* | 30 ml | 2 tbsp | 2 tbsp |
| *Can chopped tomatoes* | 400 g | 14 oz | 14 oz |
| *Vegetable stock* | 300 ml | 1/2 pt | 1 1/4 cups |
| *Mushrooms, quartered* | 100 g | 4 oz | 2 cup |
| *Salt and pepper* | | | |
| *Dried oregano or marjoram* | 2.5 ml | 1/2 tsp | 1/2 tsp |
| *Worcestershire sauce* | a dash | a dash | a dash |
| *Basil* | 2.5 ml | 1/2 tsp | 1/2 tsp |
| *Spaghetti* | 350 g | 12 oz | 3 cups |
| *To serve:* | | | |
| *Grated hard vegetarian cheese* | | | |

1. Heat the oil and fry (sauté) the garlic, onion, celery and carrots for 3 minutes, stirring.

2. Stir in the flour and cook for a further minute.

3. Add the tomatoes, stock, mushrooms, seasoning, Worcestershire sauce and herbs and stir well.

4. Bring to the boil, reduce heat and simmer gently for 10 minutes, stirring occasionally. Add the beans and cook for a further 10 minutes.

5. Meanwhile, cook spaghetti according to packet directions. Drain. Serve Volognaise sauce on a bed of spaghetti with lots of grated vegetarian hard cheese handed separately.

Preparation time: 15 minutes
Cooking time: 24 minutes

# Spinach and Cashew Nut Loaf

This loaf is equally delicious served hot with vegetables or cold with salads. For a less expensive dish, use raw peanuts instead of cashews.

| *F* Serves 4 | Metric | Imperial | American |
|---|---|---|---|
| Frozen spinach, thawed | 225 g | 8 oz | 1 cup |
| Large onion, quartered | 1 | 1 | 1 |
| Garlic clove, crushed | 1 | 1 | 1 |
| Cashew nuts | 175 g | 6 oz | 1½ cups |
| Slices wholemeal bread | 4 | 4 | 4 |
| Egg | 1 | 1 | 1 |
| Yeast extract | 5 ml | 1 tsp | 1 tsp |
| Dried mixed herbs | 1.5 ml | ¼ tsp | ¼ tsp |
| Salt and pepper | | | |

1. Squeeze out any moisture from spinach.

2. Place in a food processor and chop with the onion, garlic, nuts and bread. Alternatively pass through a coarse mincer (grinder).

3. Lightly beat egg with the yeast extract and stir into mixture with the herbs. Season lightly.

4. Turn mixture into a greased 450 g/1 lb loaf tin and cover with foil.

5. Bake at 180°C/350°F/gas mark 4 for 1 hour or until firm to the touch. Cool slightly, then turn out of the tin and serve hot or cold.

Preparation time: 10 minutes
Cooking time: 1 hour

# Stir-Fry Special

| Serves 4 | Metric | Imperial | American |
|---|---|---|---|
| Cucumber, diced | 1/2 | 1/2 | 1/2 |
| Bunch of watercress, chopped | 1 | 1 | 1 |
| Carrot, cut in matchsticks | 1 | 1 | 1 |
| Onion, sliced | 1 | 1 | 1 |
| Sliced mushrooms | 100 g | 4 oz | 2 cups |
| Flageolet beans, cooked | 100 g | 4 oz | 2/3 cup |
| Soya oil | 30 ml | 2 tbsp | 2 tbsp |
| Soy sauce | 30 ml | 2 tbsp | 2 tbsp |
| Medium sherry | 15 ml | 1 tbsp | 1 tbsp |
| Ground ginger | 1.5 ml | 1/4 tsp | 1/4 tsp |
| Chilli (chili) powder | good pinch | good pinch | good pinch |
| Demerara (light brown) sugar | 10 ml | 2 tsp | 2 tsp |
| *To serve:* | | | |
| Noodles | | | |

1. Fry (sauté) all the prepared vegetables in a large frying pan (skillet) or wok for 3 minutes, stirring.

2. Add the remaining ingredients and continue frying for 5 minutes, tossing all the time.

3. Serve hot on a bed of noodles.

Preparation time: 10 minutes
Cooking time: 8 minutes

# Surprise Potato Bake

| *M* *F* Serves 4 | Metric | Imperial | American |
|---|---|---|---|
| Potatoes, peeled and cut into small pieces | 900 g | 2 lb | 2 lb |
| Salt and pepper | | | |
| Egg, beaten | 1 | 1 | 1 |
| Soya margarine | 50 g | 2 oz | 1/4 cup |
| Skimmed milk | 45 ml | 3 tbsp | 3 tbsp |
| Onion, chopped | 1 | 1 | 1 |
| Chopped hazelnuts | 50 g | 2 oz | 1/2 cup |
| Ground cumin | 5 ml | 1 tsp | 1 tsp |
| Turmeric | 2.5 ml | 1/2 tsp | 1/2 tsp |
| Stick (rib) celery, chopped | 1 | 1 | 1 |
| Tomato purée (paste) | 15 ml | 1 tbsp | 1 tbsp |
| Tomatoes, chopped | 2 | 2 | 2 |
| Lemon juice | 5 ml | 1 tsp | 1 tsp |
| Desiccated (shredded) coconut | 75 g | 3 oz | 3/4 cup |
| To serve: | | | |
| Green beans | | | |

1. Cook the potatoes in boiling, salted water until tender (about 10-15 minutes).

2. Drain the potatoes and beat in the egg, half the margarine and the milk. Season to taste.

3. Meanwhile, melt the remaining margarine in a pan. Add onion and fry (sauté) for 3 minutes, stirring.

4. Add the hazelnuts, cumin, turmeric, celery, tomatoes, tomato purée and lemon juice and continue cooking for 5 minutes, stirring all the time. In a greased casserole dish (Dutch oven), put a layer of half the potato mixture, then all the tomato mixture, followed by the remaining potatoes. Sprinkle with coconut and bake in the oven at 190°C/375°F/ gas mark 5 for 40 minutes. Serve hot with green beans.

Preparation time: 15 minutes
Cooking time: 50-55 minutes

# Sweet and Sour Tofu

| Serves 4 | Metric | Imperial | American |
|---|---|---|---|
| *Firm tofu* | *225 g* | *8 oz* | *1 cup* |
| *Soya margarine* | *15 ml* | *1 tbsp* | *1 tbsp* |
| *Soya oil* | *15 ml* | *1 tbsp* | *1 tbsp* |
| *Sauce:* | | | |
| *Can pineapple chunks* | *320 g* | *12 oz* | *12 oz* |
| *Carrot, cut in matchsticks* | *1* | *1* | *1* |
| *Green (bell) pepper, diced* | *$^1/_2$* | *$^1/_2$* | *$^1/_2$* |
| *Ground ginger* | *2.5 ml* | *$^1/_2$ tsp* | *$^1/_2$ tsp* |
| *Demerara (light brown) sugar* | *15 ml* | *1 tbsp* | *1 tbsp* |
| *Soy sauce* | *15 ml* | *1 tbsp* | *1 tbsp* |
| *Malt vinegar* | *15 ml* | *1 tbsp* | *1 tbsp* |
| *Tomato purée (paste)* | *15 ml* | *1 tbsp* | *1 tbsp* |
| *Cornflour (cornstarch)* | *15 ml* | *1 tbsp* | *1 tbsp* |
| *Water* | *15 ml* | *1 tbsp* | *1 tbsp* |
| *To serve:* | | | |
| *Plain rice* | | | |

1. Cut the tofu into bite-sized chunks.

2. Heat the margarine and oil in a large frying pan (skillet) and  fry (sauté) the tofu for about 5 minutes until golden brown,  stirring.  Drain on kitchen paper.

3. Drain the pineapple, reserving juice. Make juice up to 300 ml/½ pt/1¼ cups with water and pour into a saucepan.

4. Add the pineapple, carrot, pepper, ginger, sugar, soy sauce, vinegar and tomato purée. Bring to the boil and simmer for 3  minutes.

5. Blend the cornflour with the water and stir into pan. Cook stirring for 2 minutes until thickened and clear.

6. Mix in the tofu and heat through. Serve on a bed of rice.

Preparation time: 15 minutes
Cooking time: 10 minutes

# Two Bean Casserole

The combination of honey and mustard gives this casserole an  unusual flavour.

| *F* Serves 4 | Metric | Imperial | American |
|---|---|---|---|
| *Soya margarine* | *50 g* | *2 oz* | *$1/_4$ cup* |
| *Onion* | *1* | *1* | *1* |
| *Haricot (navy) beans, cooked* | *175 g* | *6 oz* | *$1^1/_2$ cups* |
| *Red kidney beans, cooked* | *175 g* | *6 oz* | *$1^1/_2$ cups* |
| *Can chopped tomatoes* | *400 g* | *14 oz* | *14 oz* |
| *Clear honey* | *30 ml* | *2 tbsp* | *2 tbsp* |
| *Grainy mustard* | *5 ml* | *1 tsp* | *1 tsp* |
| *Salt and pepper* | | | |
| *Pumpkin seeds* | *15 ml* | *1 tbsp* | *1 tbsp* |
| *To serve:* | | | |
| *Green tagliatelle* | | | |

1. Melt the margarine in a pan and fry (sauté) the onion for 3 minutes, stirring.

2. Add remaining ingredients, bring to the boil, cover and cook  for about 8 minutes or until the beans are bathed in a rich sauce.

3. Serve hot with green tagliatelle.

Preparation time: 3 minutes
Cooking time: 11 minutes

# Vegetable Burgers

The children will love to help you make these delicious burgers. For a variation, substitute half the oats with 50 g/ 2 oz/½ cup  mixed chopped nuts. Alternatively, top with a slice of vegetarian Cheddar  after cooking and flash under a hot grill (broiler) before  serving.

| *F* Serves 4 | Metric | Imperial | American |
|---|---|---|---|
| Rolled oats | 100 g | 4 oz | 1 cup |
| Wholemeal (graham) flour | 75 g | 3 oz | ¾ cup |
| Sticks (ribs) celery, finely chopped | 2 | 2 | 2 |
| Carrots, grated | 3 | 3 | 3 |
| Grated vegetarian Cheddar cheese | 50 g | 2 oz | ½ cup |
| Onion, finely chopped | ½ | ½ | ½ |
| Tomato purée (paste) | 15 ml | 1 tbsp | 1 tbsp |
| Soy sauce | 15 ml | 1 tbsp | 1 tbsp |
| Dried mixed herbs | 5 ml | 1 tsp | 1 tsp |
| Salt and pepper | | | |
| Egg, beaten | 1 | 1 | 1 |
| Oil for frying | | | |
| To serve: | | | |
| Baps, ketchup (catsup), mustard and salad. | | | |

1. Mix all the ingredients, except the oil, together and shape into  burgers - not too thick.

2. Fry (sauté) in hot oil for 5 minutes, turning once.

3. Drain on kitchen paper and serve in baps with ketchup, mustard  and salad.

**Note:**
This recipe is very versatile and can be used as a cottage pie mixture or formed into sausages or a loaf.

Preparation time: 15 minutes
Cooking time: 5 minutes

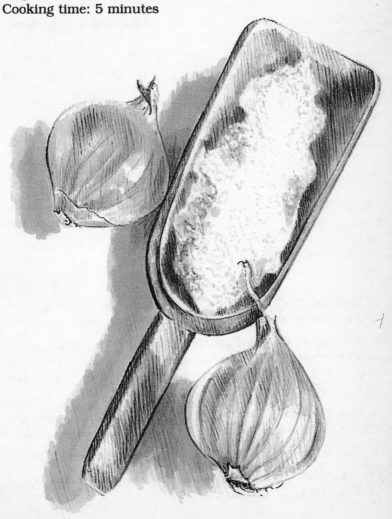

# Vegetarian Kedgeree

My fish-eating friends say this is just as delicious as their version of this traditional dish.

| *M* *F* Serves 4 | Metric | Imperial | American |
|---|---|---|---|
| Soya margarine | 75 g | 3 oz | 1/3 cup |
| Onion, chopped | 1 | 1 | 1 |
| Yellow split peas, soaked overnight in cold water | 225 g | 8 oz | 1 1/3 cups |
| Brown long grain rice | 275 g | 10 oz | 1 1/4 cups |
| Grated nutmeg | pinch | pinch | pinch |
| Salt and pepper | | | |
| Hard- boiled (hard-cooked) eggs, quartered | 4 | 4 | 4 |
| Skimmed milk | 150 ml | 1/4 pt | 2/3 cup |
| To garnish: | | | |
| Chopped parsley | 45 ml | 3 tbsp | 3 tbsp |
| To serve: | | | |
| Poached tomatoes | | | |

1. Melt the 50 g/2 oz/¼ cup soya margarine in a large pan. Add the onion and fry (sauté) for 3 minutes, stirring.

2. Add the drained yellow split peas, rice and just enough water to cover. Bring to the boil and cook for about 30 minutes or until the split peas and rice are tender and have absorbed all the liquid.

3. Add the eggs, the remaining margarine, milk and parsley. Stir well and simmer for 4 minutes, stirring occasionally.

4. Garnish with parsley and serve hot with poached tomatoes.

Preparation time: 5 minutes, plus soaking of split peas
Cooking time: 37 minutes

CHAPTER 3

# VEGETABLE ACCOMPANIMENTS AND SALADS

**L**ots of people, especially children, find plain vegetables boring. So here is a range of deliciously different combinations of textures and flavours, both hot and cold, that will tickle even the most jaded palate.

Many of the accompanying vegetable dishes would make nourishing main meals with the addition of some extra protein, e.g. cooked beans or lentils, hard-boiled eggs, cheese or nuts, and served with a potato dish.

# Baked Spiced Carrots

This is always a colourful addition to any meal

| *M* Serves 4 | Metric | Imperial | American |
|---|---|---|---|
| *Carrots, sliced* | *750 g* | *1½ lbs* | *1½ lbs* |
| *Soya margarine* | *25 g* | *1 oz* | *2 tbsp* |
| *Grated rind and juice of* | | | |
| *orange* | *1* | *1* | *1* |
| *Ground ginger* | *pinch* | *pinch* | *pinch* |
| *Nutmeg* | *pinch* | *pinch* | *pinch* |
| *Salt and pepper* | | | |
| *To garnish:* | | | |
| *Chopped fresh parsley* | *15 ml* | *1 tbsp* | *1 tbsp* |

1. Put all the ingredients except parsley in an ovenproof dish.

2. Cover and bake at 190°C/375°F/gas mark 5 for 45 minutes or until just tender.

3. Sprinkle with chopped parsley before serving.

Preparation time: 5 minutes
Cooking time: 45 minutes

# Broad Beans with Walnut Sauce

This dish could be made with runner beans if preferred.

| *M* *F* Serves 4 | Metric | Imperial | American |
|---|---|---|---|
| *Fresh shelled or frozen broad (lima) beans* | *450 g* | *1 lb* | *4 cups* |
| *Soya margarine* | *15 g* | *¹/₂ oz* | *1 tbsp* |
| *Wholemeal (graham) flour* | *15 g* | *¹/₂ oz* | *2 tbsp* |
| *Vegetable stock* | *300 ml* | *¹/₂ pt* | *1¹/₄ cups* |
| *Chopped walnuts* | *50 g* | *2 oz* | *¹/₂ cup* |
| *Salt and pepper* | | | |

1. Cook the broad beans in plenty of boiling water until just tender. Drain.

2. Melt the margarine in a pan, add the flour and cook for 1 minute.

3. Gradually blend in the stock, bring to the boil and cook for 2 minutes, stirring.

4. Add salt and pepper to taste and the walnuts and pour over the beans.

Preparation time: 5 minutes
Cooking time: 15 minutes

# Broccoli in Tomato Sauce

This tomato sauce is very easy to make and any cooked vegetable, such as courgettes, red or green peppers, leeks, mushrooms, marrow, sweetcorn, celery, cabbage or cooked pulses could be added to it to make a change.

| *M* *F* Serves 4 | Metric | Imperial | American |
|---|---|---|---|
| Soya oil | 25 g | 1 oz | 2 tbsp |
| Onion, chopped | 1 | 1 | 1 |
| Wholemeal (graham) flour | 25 g | 1 oz | 1/4 cup |
| Can chopped tomatoes | 400 g | 14 oz | 14 oz |
| Salt and pepper | | | |
| Sugar | 2.5 ml | 1/2 tsp | 1/2 tsp |
| Cooked broccoli spears | 750 g | 1 1/2 lbs | 1 1/2 lbs |
| Grated vegetarian Cheddar cheese | 100 g | 4 oz | 1 cup |
| *To garnish:* | | | |
| Few toasted flaked almonds | | | |

1. Heat the oil and fry (sauté) the onion for 3 minutes, until soft.

2. Stir in the flour and cook for 1 minute.

3. Add the tomatoes, salt, pepper and sugar and cover. Bring to the boil, reduce heat and simmer for 5 minutes, stirring occasionally.

4. Put the broccoli in a greased ovenproof dish, pour tomato sauce over and sprinkle with grated cheese. Bake at 190°C/375°F/gas mark 5 for 30 minutes or until topping is golden and bubbling. Sprinkle with almonds and serve.

Preparation time: 5 minutes
Cooking time: 38 minutes

# Carrot and Swede Cream

You can use any combination of root vegetables for this dish.

| Serves 4 | Metric | Imperial | American |
|---|---|---|---|
| *Mixed carrots and swede (rutabaga), diced* | *450 g* | *1 lb* | *4 cups* |
| *Quark* | *100 g* | *4 oz* | *1/2 cup* |
| *Soya oil* | *15 ml* | *1 tbsp* | *1 tbsp* |
| *Salt and pepper* | | | |
| *To garnish:* | | | |
| *Toasted sesame seeds* | | | |

1. Boil the vegetables in lightly salted water until just tender.

2. Drain and put with remaining ingredients, except sesame seeds, into a food processor or blender. Process for 2 minutes.

3. Reheat and sprinkle with toasted sesame seeds to garnish before serving.

Preparation time: 8 minutes
Cooking time: 5-10 minutes

# Celery and Cabbage Casserole

Served with a light cheese or egg dish and jacket potatoes, this makes a nourishing meal.

| Serves 4 | Metric | Imperial | American |
|---|---|---|---|
| Soya margarine | 100 g | 4 oz | ¹/₂ cup |
| Small onion, chopped | 1 | 1 | 1 |
| Small celery head, sliced | 1 | 1 | 1 |
| Small white cabbage, shredded | ¹/₂ | ¹/₂ | ¹/₂ |
| Wholemeal flour | 25 g | 1 oz | 2 tbsp |
| Skimmed milk | 300 ml | ¹/₂ pt | 1¹/₄ cups |
| Salt and pepper | | | |
| Breadcrumbs | 25 g | 1 oz | ¹/₂ cup |
| Sunflower seeds or peanuts | 25 g | 1 oz | ¹/₄ cup |

1. Melt half the margarine in a pan and fry (sauté) the chopped onion for 3 minutes, stirring.

2. Add the celery and cook for a further 2 minutes.

3. Add the cabbage, cover, and continue cooking gently for 5 minutes, stirring occasionally to prevent sticking.

4. Drain, reserving juice and turn into an ovenproof dish.

5. To make the white sauce, melt 25 g/1 oz/2 tbsp of the remaining margarine in a pan. Stir in the flour and cook for 1 minute. Gradually stir in the milk and reserved cabbage juice, bring to the boil and cook for 2 minutes until thickened.

6. Season to taste and pour sauce over vegetables. Sprinkle with breadcrumbs and sunflower seeds or peanuts.

7. Dot with remaining margarine and cook in oven at 180°C/350°F/gas mark 4 for 20 minutes.

Preparation time: 10 minutes
Cooking time: 32 minutes

# Coleslaw

There are many, many variations of this lovely accompaniment. This is my favourite, but adjust it to suit your particular taste.

| Serves 4 | Metric | Imperial | American |
|---|---|---|---|
| *White cabbage, shredded* | *100 g* | *4 oz* | *1 cup* |
| *Sticks (ribs) celery, chopped* | *2* | *2* | *2* |
| *Sultanas (golden raisins)* | *50 g* | *2 oz* | *¹/₃ cup* |
| *Walnuts, chopped* | *50 g* | *2 oz* | *¹/₂ cup* |
| *Chopped (snipped) chives* | *15 ml* | *1 tbsp* | *1 tbsp* |
| *Salt and pepper* | | | |
| *Mayonnaise (see page 152)* | *60 ml* | *4 tbsp* | *4 tbsp* |
| ***To garnish:*** | | | |
| *Sesame seeds* | | | |

1. Mix all the ingredients together well. Turn into a serving bowl.

2. Sprinkle with a generous helping of sesame seeds to garnish.

Preparation time: 8 minutes

# Courgettes with Herbs

Tarragon and courgettes (zucchini) complement each other perfectly.

| *M* Serves 4 | Metric | Imperial | American |
|---|---|---|---|
| *Soya margarine* | *25 g* | *1 oz* | *2 tbsp* |
| *Courgettes (zucchini), sliced or for a change quartered lengthwise* | *750 g* | *1¹/₂ lbs* | *1¹/₂ lbs* |
| *Salt and pepper* | | | |
| *Tarragon, chopped* | *15 ml* | *1 tbsp* | *1 tbsp* |

1. Put the courgettes into a large pan of boiling water and simmer for 4 minutes. Drain.

2. Add the remaining ingredients, stir well and heat through thoroughly. Serve immediately.

Preparation time: 4 minutes
Cooking time: 8-10 minutes

# Creamy Braised Lettuce

| Serves 4 | Metric | Imperial | American |
|---|---|---|---|
| Onion, finely chopped | 1 | 1 | 1 |
| Hearty round lettuce, quartered | 1 | 1 | 1 |
| Soya margarine | 25 g | 1 oz | 2 tbsp |
| Vegetable stock | 150 ml | 1/4 pt | 2/3 cup |
| Pepper | | | |
| Cornflour (cornstarch) | 10 ml | 2 tsp | 2 tsp |
| Water | 30 ml | 2 tbsp | 2 tbsp |
| Low fat single (light) cream | 150 ml | 1/4 pt | 2/3 cup |
| Chopped (snipped) chives | 15 ml | 1 tbsp | 1 tbsp |
| Toasted flaked almonds | 15 ml | 1 tbsp | 1 tbsp |

1. Fry (sauté) the onion and lettuce in the melted margarine for 2 minutes, turning lettuce over after 1 minute.

2. Add the stock and a little pepper, cover and simmer for 5 minutes. Lift lettuce out of pan and place in a warm dish. Keep warm.

3. Blend the cornflour with the water. Stir into pan and bring to the boil, stirring until thickened. Simmer for 2 minutes.

4. Stir in the cream and chives and heat through gently. Pour over lettuce and sprinkle toasted almonds over.

Preparation time: 5 minutes
Cooking time: 12 minutes

# Creamy Sprouts with Paprika

| *M* Serves 4 | Metric | Imperial | American |
|---|---|---|---|
| *Brussels sprouts, trimmed and bottoms slit* | *450 ml* | *1 lb* | *1 lb* |
| *Vegetable stock* | *150 ml* | *¼ pt* | *⅔ cup* |
| *Paprika* | *10 ml* | *2 tsp* | *2 tsp* |
| *Tomato purée (paste)* | *5 ml* | *1 tsp* | *1 tsp* |
| *Salt and pepper* | | | |
| *Soya margarine* | *25 g* | *1 oz* | *2 tbsp* |
| *Crème fraiche* | *150 ml* | *¼ pt* | *⅔ cup* |

1. Put all the ingredients except the crème fraiche, into a large bowl, cover with cling film and microwave on high for 12 minutes, stirring once.

2. Swirl in crème fraiche and serve.

Preparation time: 5 minutes
Cooking time: 12 minutes

# Curried Cabbage

| *M* Serves 4 | Metric | Imperial | American |
|---|---|---|---|
| Cabbage, chopped, thick<br>    stalk removed | 1 | 1 | 1 |
| Soya margarine | 50 g | 2 oz | 1/4 cup |
| Chutney (see page 153) | 10 ml | 2 tsp | 2 tsp |
| Mild curry powder | 5 ml | 1 tsp | 1 tsp |
| Lemon juice | 15 ml | 1 tbsp | 1 tbsp |
| Salt and pepper | | | |
| **To garnish:** | | | |
| Desiccated (shredded)<br>    coconut | | | |

1. Cook the cabbage in boiling, lightly salted water until just tender, but not soggy. Drain.

2. Stir in remaining ingredients. Leave to stand for 5 minutes.

3. Reheat then turn into a serving dish and garnish with desiccated coconut.

Preparation time: 5 minutes
Cooking time: 5 minutes

# Curried Sweetcorn Salad

This salad is ideal when you have unexpected guests as most of the ingredients are usually to be found in the store cupboard.

| *F* Serves 4 | Metric | Imperial | American |
|---|---|---|---|
| *Cans sweetcorn (corn) drained* | *2 x 320 g* | *2 x 12 oz* | *2 x 12 oz* |
| *Chopped (snipped) chives* | *15 ml* | *1 tbsp* | *1 tbsp* |
| *Mayonnaise (see page 152)* | *30 ml* | *2 tbsp* | *2 tbsp* |
| *Lemon juice* | *15 ml* | *1 tbsp* | *1 tbsp* |
| *Chutney (see page 153)* | *30 ml* | *2 tbsp* | *2 tbsp* |
| *Salt and pepper* | | | |
| *Paprika* | *10 ml* | *2 tsp* | *2 tsp* |
| *Mild curry powder* | *15 ml* | *1 tbsp* | *1 tbsp* |
| *Chopped fresh parsley* | *15 ml* | *1 tbsp* | *1 tbsp* |

1. Mix all the ingredients, except parsley, together in a bowl. Garnish with chopped parsley and serve or chill until required.

Preparation time: 3 minutes

# Leek and Sprout Hotpot

| *M* Serves 4 | Metric | Imperial | American |
|---|---|---|---|
| Potatoes, scrubbed and sliced thinly | 450 g | 1 lb | 1 lb |
| Salt | | | |
| Brussels sprouts, trimmed and bottoms slit | 450 g | 1 lb | 1 lb |
| Leek, sliced lengthways, cut into 2.5 cm/1 in lengths | 1 | 1 | 1 |
| Vegetable stock | 150 ml | 1/4 pt | 2/3 cup |
| Freshly–made mustard | 5 ml | 1 tsp | 1 tsp |
| Chopped tarragon | 5 ml | 1 tsp | 1 tsp |
| Grated vegetarian Cheddar cheese | 50 g | 2 oz | 1/2 cup |

1. Cook the potato slices in boiling, lightly salted water for 4 minutes. Drain.

2. Put the sprouts and leek in a flameproof casserole. Add the stock, bring to the boil and simmer gently for 3 minutes. Stir in the mustard and tarragon.

3. Lay the potato slices on top. Cover with cheese. Bake at 190°C/375°F/gas mark 5 for about 45 minutes until golden and just cooked through. Serve hot.

Preparation time: 10 minutes
Cooking time: 52 minutes

# Mixed Bean Salad

This is nourishing enough for a main course, simply serve with crusty bread.

| Serves 4 | Metric | Imperial | American |
|---|---|---|---|
| Red kidney beans, cooked | 100 g | 4 oz | 1 cup |
| Butter beans, cooked | 100 g | 4 oz | 1 cup |
| Haricot (navy) beans, cooked | 100 g | 4 oz | 1 cup |
| Broad (lima) beans, cooked | 225 g | 8 oz | 2 cups |
| French beans, cut in thirds, cooked | 225 g | 8 oz | 2 cups |
| Small onion, finely chopped | 1 | 1 | 1 |
| **Dressing:** | | | |
| Garlic clove, crushed | 1 | 1 | 1 |
| Soya oil | 45 ml | 3 tbsp | 3 tbsp |
| Cider vinegar | 15 ml | 1 tbsp | 1 tbsp |
| Salt and pepper | | | |
| **To garnish:** | | | |
| Hard-boiled (hard-cooked) eggs, quartered | 2 | 2 | 2 |

1. Mix all the beans together in a large salad bowl.

2. Scatter the onion over.

3. Put dressing ingredients in a screw-topped jar and shake well until blended.

4. Pour over the beans and toss well. Arrange quartered eggs attractively in the centre to garnish.

Preparation time: 15 minutes

# Mushroom and Beansprout Salad

Add a tablespoon of sweetcorn (corn) to this recipe for colour.

| Serves 4 | Metric | Imperial | American |
|---|---|---|---|
| *Mushrooms, thinly sliced* | *225 g* | *8 oz* | *4 cups* |
| *Worcestershire sauce* | *5 ml* | *1 tsp* | *1 tsp* |
| *Soy sauce* | *30 ml* | *2 tbsp* | *2 tbsp* |
| *Salt and pepper* | | | |
| *Beansprouts, roughly chopped* | *225 g* | *8 oz* | *2 cups* |
| *Ground ginger* | *good pinch* | *good pinch* | *good pinch* |

1. Put the mushrooms into a large bowl and sprinkle with Worcestershire sauce, soy sauce, salt and pepper. Leave for 1 hour.

2. Add the beansprouts, sprinkle with ginger and stir in well.

Preparation time: 3 minutes plus standing time

# Pat's Perfect Rice

Measuring the rice and water in the same jug gives you exactly the right proportions if you use 1 jug of rice to 2 jugs of water. A 1 pint jug take about 225 g/8 oz rice.

| *M* *F* Serves 4 | Metric | Imperial | American |
|---|---|---|---|
| *Jug of easy-cook brown rice* | *1* | *1* | *1* |
| *Salt and pepper* | | | |
| *Bay leaf* | *1* | *1* | *1* |
| *Jugfuls of boiling water* | | | |
| *(use same jug)* | *2* | *2* | *2* |

This method is recommended by my mother for producing perfectly cooked brown rice.

**Method 1:**

1. Put rice, salt, pepper, bay leaf and water in large bowl and leave for 1 hour.

2. Heat through in the microwave on high for 4 minutes. Remove bay leaf and serve.

**Method 2:**

1. Place all ingredients in a saucepan. Cover with a tight–fitting lid.

2. Bring to the boil. Reduce heat as low as possible and cook for 25-30 minutes.

3. Remove from heat. Do not take off lid. Leave to stand for 5 minutes. Fluff up and serve.

Preparation time: 2 minutes
Cooking time: method 1: 1 hr 4 minutes
method 2: 25-30 minutes

# Red Cabbage with Apple and Onion Bake

Red cabbage is one of my favourite vegetables and it gives such a good colour contrast to green vegetables.

| *M* *F* Serves 4 | Metric | Imperial | American |
|---|---|---|---|
| Red cabbage, washed and chopped | 450 g | 1 lb | 1 lb |
| Onion, chopped | 1 | 1 | 1 |
| Eating (dessert) apple, chopped | 1 | 1 | 1 |
| Salt and pepper | | | |
| Vinegar | 30 ml | 2 tbsp | 2 tbsp |
| Soya margarine | 25 g | 1 oz | 2 tbsp |
| Sultanas (golden raisins) (optional) | 50 g | 2 oz | 1/3 cup |

1. Put all ingredients into a large casserole (Dutch oven).

2. Bake in a slow oven 160°C/325°F/gas mark 3 for up to 2 hours. Alternatively, cook very gently on top of the stove, stirring occasionally, for about 45 minutes. Add a little water if necessary.

Preparation time: 10 minutes
Cooking time: 45 minutes or 2 hours

# Spicy Savoy with Apple

| *M* Serves 4 | Metric | Imperial | American |
|---|---|---|---|
| Soya oil | 15 ml 1 | tbsp | 1 tbsp |
| Onion, chopped | 1 | 1 | 1 |
| Savoy cabbage, washed and shredded, thick stalk removed | 1 | 1 | 1 |
| Eating (dessert) apples, sliced | 2 | 2 | 2 |
| Worcestershire sauce | 15 ml | 1 tbsp | 1 tbsp |
| Tomato purée (paste) | 15 ml | 1 tbsp | 1 tbsp |
| Vegetable stock | 150 ml | 1/4 pt | 2/3 cup |
| Allspice powder | 5 ml | 1 tsp | 1 tsp |
| Cloves | 2 | 2 | 2 |
| Salt and pepper | | | |

1. Heat the oil in a large pan. Add the onion and fry (sauté) for 2 minutes.

2. Add the cabbage and apple and toss over a gentle heat until cabbage begins to soften.

3. Blend Worcestershire sauce with the tomato purée and stock.

4. Pour over the cabbage and add spice, cloves and a little salt and pepper. Bring to the boil.

5. Cover with a tight-fitting lid, reduce heat and simmer for 12-15 minutes or until tender, tossing occasionally.

6. Remove cloves before serving.

Preparation time: 10 minutes
Cooking time: 15-20 minutes

# Tomato, Onion and Chive Salad

| Serves 4 | Metric | Imperial | American |
|---|---|---|---|
| *Onions, sliced* | *2* | *2* | *2* |
| *Salt* | | | |
| *Tomatoes, sliced* | *6* | *6* | *6* |
| *Chopped (snipped) chives* | *10 ml* | *2 tsp* | *2 tsp* |
| ***French dressing:*** | | | |
| *Pepper* | *pinch* | *pinch* | *pinch* |
| *Mustard powder* | *30 ml* | *2 tbsp* | *2 tbsp* |
| *Soya oil* | *30 ml* | *2 tbsp* | *2 tbsp* |
| *Vinegar* | *30 ml* | *2 tbsp* | *2 tbsp* |
| *Caster (superfine) sugar* | *pinch* | *pinch* | *pinch* |

1. Put the sliced onions on a plate, sprinkle with salt and leave for 30 minutes. Rinse thoroughly and pat dry on kitchen paper. (This process softens the onions and takes away the strong taste.)

2. Place layers of onions and tomatoes in a flat dish, sprinkle with chives.

3. Put dressing ingredients in a screw-topped jar with a pinch of salt. Shake vigorously, then pour over salad. Leave to stand for 10 minutes before serving.

Preparation time: 5 minutes plus standing time

# Watercress, Orange and Onion Salad

| Serves 4 | Metric | Imperial | American |
|---|---|---|---|
| *Bunch watercress* | *1* | *1* | *1* |
| *Oranges* | *2* | *2* | *2* |
| *Small onion, sliced into rings* | *1* | *1* | *1* |
| *Soya or olive oil* | *30 ml* | *2 tbsp* | *2 tbsp* |
| *Lemon juice* | *5 ml* | *1 tsp* | *1 tsp* |
| *Salt and pepper* | | | |

1. Trim any feathery stalks off the watercress. Arrange the leaves attractively in a shallow dish.

2. Grate rind and squeeze juice from one of the oranges into a bowl.

3. Remove all rind and pith from remaining orange and cut into slices. Cut each slice in half and arrange attractively over the watercress.

4. Scatter onion rings on top.

5. Add oil, lemon juice and a little salt and pepper to orange rind and juice. Whisk until well blended. Pour over salad and serve.

Preparation time: 5 minutes

# CHAPTER 4

# DESSERTS

**M**ost of us have to admit to liking luscious sweet puddings, but feel guilty if we attack the chocolate mousse or fresh cream gateau too often. In this section, there is a whole selection of recipes which are lower in sugar and higher in nutrients than the average pud, but equally sumptuous. You can, of course, continue using all your usual pudding recipes, provided you don't use animal fats.

# Apple and Coconut Pie

| Serves 4 | Metric | Imperial | American |
|---|---|---|---|
| Soya margarine | 25 g | 1 oz | 2 tbsp |
| Eating (dessert) apples, sliced | 750 g | 1½ lbs | 1½ lbs |
| Demerara (light brown) sugar | 45 ml | 3 tbsp | 3 tbsp |
| Mixed (apple pie) spice | 5 ml | 1 tsp | 1 tsp |
| Dates, stoned (pitted) and chopped | 100 g | 4 oz | ⅔ cup |
| Egg white | 100 g | 4 oz | ⅔ cup |
| Desiccated (shredded) coconut | 50 g | 2 oz | ½ cup |
| To serve: | | | |
| Crème fraiche | | | |

1. Melt the margarine in a saucepan. Add the apples, spice and half the sugar. Cover and cook gently, stirring occasionally, for 5 minutes.

2. Stir in the dates and place in a greased pie dish.

3. Whisk the egg white until stiff and add remaining sugar and coconut. Continue whisking until stiff again and spread mixture over fruit using a fork.

4. Bake for 20 minutes at 180°C/350°F/gas mark 4 and serve warm with crème fraiche.

Preparation time: 15 minutes
Cooking time: 25 minutes

# Boozy Carob Ice

This dessert is very rich and tastes as wickedly sinful as any chocolate dessert.

| *M* *F* Serves 4 | Metric | Imperial | American |
|---|---|---|---|
| *Soya margarine* | *100 g* | *4 oz* | *¹/₂ cup* |
| *Carob chips* | *175 g* | *6 oz* | *1 cup* |
| *Plain wholemeal biscuits (cookies) crushed* | *200 g* | *7 oz* | *scant 1 cup* |
| *Eggs, beaten* | *3* | *3* | *3* |
| *Sweet sherry or coffee liqueur* | *30 ml* | *2 tbsp* | *2 tbsp* |
| *Whipped low fat cream* | *150 ml* | *¹/₄ pt* | *²/₃ cup* |
| *To decorate:* | | | |
| *A little extra whipped low fat cream and grated nutmeg (optional)* | | | |

1. Put the margarine and carob in a large pan and heat gently, stirring until melted.

2. Stir in the biscuits, eggs and sherry. Leave to cool and then fold in the cream.

3. Put mixture in a greased mould or pudding basin.

4. Freeze for at least 4 hours before serving.

5. Turn out and pipe a little extra cream, if liked, on top and then sprinkle with a little grated nutmeg.

**Note:**
To turn out frozen desserts, just stand them briefly in a bowl of
boiling water, cover with a plate and invert quickly. Remove the mould and refreeze immediately to reharden the edges if necessary.

Preparation time: 10 minutes plus cooling and freezing time.

# Caramel Ice Cream

This is extremely easy to make, tastes delicious and doesn't contain all the preservatives and additives that are found in commercially–prepared ice cream. It keeps well and could be served just as it is or made into a bombe for a special occasion (see page 115). Always allow home made ice cream to thaw in the fridge for about 30 minutes before using, to soften slightly.

| *M* *F* Serves 4 | Metric | Imperial | American |
|---|---|---|---|
| *Demerara (light brown) sugar* | 100 g | 4 oz | ¹/₂ cup |
| *Water* | 150 ml | ¹/₄ pt | ²/₃ cup |
| *Soya margarine* | 25 g | 1 oz | 2 tbsp |
| *Lemon juice* | 10 ml | 2 tsp | 2 tsp |
| *Arrowroot, blended with a little water* | 10 ml | 2 tsp | 2 tsp |
| *Can evaporated milk, chilled in the fridge overnight* | 400 g | 14 oz | 14 oz |
| *Real vanilla essence (extract)* | 2.5 ml | ¹/₂ tsp | ¹/₂ tsp |

1. Put the sugar, water, margarine and lemon juice into a saucepan and heat gently, stirring until melted.

2. Add the blended arrowroot, and cook, stirring, until thickened. Cool.

3. Whisk the evaporated milk until thick and creamy and fold in the sauce and vanilla essence.

4. Pour into a container and put into the freezer. Whisk after 1 hour and return to the freezer. Whisk again after another hour and freeze until firm.

Preparation time: 10 minutes plus cooling and freezing time
Cooking time: 5 minutes

# Carob and Caramel Bombe

Always an impressive dessert, but very easy to make.

| *M* *F* Serves 4 | Metric | Imperial | American |
|---|---|---|---|
| *Quantity Caramel Ice Cream (see page 114)* | *1* | *1* | *1* |
| *Quantity Carob Chip Ice Cream (see page 116)* | *1* | *1* | *1* |
| **To decorate:** | | | |
| *Carob chips and toasted flaked almonds* | | | |

1.  Make the ice creams. After stirring them for the second time during freezing, use the caramel one to line the base and sides of an ice cream mould or pudding basin.

2.  Freeze for 30 minutes then fill the centre with the carob ice cream, pressing down firmly.

3.  Freeze until firm.

4.  Dip mould into a bowl of very hot water, turn out and decorate with carob chips and toasted, flaked almonds.

Preparation time: 15 minutes plus cooling and freezing

# Carob Chip Ice Cream

When used in cooking or mixed with other ingredients, carob is an excellent substitute for chocolate. It is full of vitamins and minerals, has fewer calories and a higher fibre content than cocoa. Carob is naturally sweeter too, so doesn't need the vast quantities of refined sugar that are added to cocoa to make chocolate. One of the most important advantages of carob must be that it is caffeine–and theobromine–free. It doesn't cause migraine or spots and is better for your teeth. Nowadays, carob is widely available, if not at your local supermarket, then at the health food shop.

| *M* *F* Serves 4 | Metric | Imperial | American |
|---|---|---|---|
| *Sifted carob powder* | *30 ml* | *2 tbsp* | *2 tbsp* |
| *Carob chips* | *30 ml* | *2 tbsp* | *2 tbsp* |

1. Follow the recipe for Caramel Ice Cream (see page 114), but fold the carob powder and chips into the sauce before folding in the whisked evaporated milk.

Preparation time: 12 minutes plus cooling and freezing

# Carob and Orange Baked Alaska

| Serves 4 | Metric | Imperial | American |
|---|---|---|---|
| *Slices of carob cake* | 6 | 6 | 6 |
| *Pure orange juice* | 150 ml | ¼ pt | ⅔ cup |
| *Oranges, peeled and chopped* | 3 | 3 | 3 |
| *Egg whites* | 3 | 3 | 3 |
| *Caster (superfine) sugar* | 75 g | 3 oz | ⅓ cup |
| *Quantity Carob Chip Ice Cream (see page 116)* | | | |

1. In a greased, shallow, ovenproof glass dish, place the slices of cake and soak with orange juice.

2. Sprinkle the chopped fruit over the top.

3. Whisk the egg whites until stiff and add sugar. Continue whisking until stiff again.

4. Pile spoonfuls or scoops of the ice cream on to the fruit and cake base and cover completely with the meringue.

5. Bake in a very hot oven 240°C/475°F/gas mark 9 for 5 minutes until meringue is just turning golden. Serve immediately.

Preparation time: 8 minutes
Cooking time: 5 minutes

# Carob and Pear Microwave Gateau

This gateau could be served just on its own for tea, but filled with fresh fruit and decorated with carob chips and whipped low fat cream or crème fraiche, it makes a delicious dessert.

| *M* Serves 4 | Metric | Imperial | American |
|---|---|---|---|
| **Cake:** | | | |
| Wholemeal self-raising (Self-rising) flour | 150 g | 5 oz | 1¼ cups |
| Carob powder | 15 ml | 1 tbsp | 1 tbsp |
| Soya margarine | 175 g | 6 oz | ¾ cup |
| Sugar | 175 g | 6 oz | ¾ cup |
| Eggs | 3 | 3 | 3 |
| Skimmed milk | 45 ml | 3 tbsp | 3 tbsp |
| Currants or sultanas (golden raisins) | 30 ml | 2 tbsp | 2 tbsp |
| **Filling:** | | | |
| Whipped low fat cream or crème fraiche | 150 ml | ¼ pt | ⅔ cup |
| Ripe pears, peeled and chopped | 2 | 2 | 2 |
| **To decorate:** | | | |
| Carob chips | | | |

1.  Grease an 18 cm/7 in deep, straight-sided soufflé dish.

2.  Beat all ingredients in a bowl until well mixed. Add extra milk if necessary to give a soft "dropping" consistency.

3. Spoon mixture into the prepared dish and microwave on high for $7^1/_2$ minutes.

4. Leave to stand for 10 minutes, then turn out on to a wire rack to cool.

5. Split and fill with half the cream and the pears. Pipe or spread remaining cream over and decorate with carob chips. Chill until ready to serve.

Preparation time: 10 minutes plus cooling and chilling time
Cooking time: $7^1/_2$ minutes

# Chestnut Gateau

People don't believe me when I tell them how low the fat and sugar content are in this recipe; the cream decoration can be omitted to keep it even lower. It makes a lovely birthday cake for an adult if you happen to be entertaining them on their special day. Decorate the cake with their name 'written' on with cherries, angelica or nuts.

| *M* *F* Serves 4 | Metric | Imperial | American |
|---|---|---|---|
| Carob chips | 225 g | 8 oz | 2 cups |
| Skimmed milk | 30 ml | 2 tbsp | 2 tbsp |
| Can unsweetened chestnut purée | 430 g | 15$\frac{1}{2}$ oz | 15$\frac{1}{2}$ oz |
| Flaked almonds | 100 g | 4 oz | 1 cup |
| Dash of rum or sherry | | | |
| Low fat whipping cream | 150 ml | $\frac{1}{4}$ pt | $\frac{2}{3}$ cup |
| **To decorate:** | | | |
| Carob chips | | | |

1. Put the carob and milk in a pan and melt over a gentle heat, stirring until carob melts.

2. Beat in the chestnut purée, flaked almonds and sherry.

3. Spread into an 18 cm/7 in greased, loose-bottomed cake tin. Chill overnight or preferably freeze.

4. Remove from tin and pipe or spoon cream substitute over the top and sides and decorate with carob chips.

Preparation time: 6 minutes plus chilling time

# Fruit Temptation

| Serves 4 | Metric | Imperial | American |
|---|---|---|---|
| *Mixed fresh fruit, chopped* | *225 g* | *8 oz* | *8 oz* |
| *Half fat cottage cheese* | *100 g* | *4 oz* | *$^1/_2$ cup* |
| *Clear honey* | *15 ml* | *1 tbsp* | *1 tbsp* |
| *Desiccated (shredded)* | | | |
| *    coconut* | *150 g* | *5 oz* | *1$^1/_4$ cups* |
| *Wholemeal (graham) flour* | *25 g* | *1 oz* | *$^1/_4$ cup* |
| *Sugar* | *25 g* | *1 oz* | *2 tbsp* |
| *Soya margarine, melted* | *50 g* | *2 oz* | *$^1/_4$ cup* |
| ***To serve:*** | | | |
| *Thick natural (plain) yoghurt* | | | |

1. Put fruit in a greased ovenproof dish.

2. Spread cottage cheese over and drizzle honey on top.

3. Mix together coconut, flour, sugar and melted margarine. Spread over cottage cheese to cover completely.

4. Bake for 20 minutes at 180°C/350°F/gas mark 4.

5. Stand for 5 minutes before serving with thick yoghurt.

Preparation time: 10 minutes
Cooking time: 20 minutes

# Grape and Apricot Snow

Vary the fruits in this very simple dessert.

| Serves 4 | Metric | Imperial | American |
|---|---|---|---|
| *Egg whites* | *3* | *3* | *3* |
| *Low fat natural (plain) yoghurt with apricots* | *450 ml* | *³/₄ pt* | *2 cups* |
| *Black grapes, halved and seeded (pitted)* | *225 g* | *8 oz* | *1¹/₃ cups* |
| *Green grapes, halved and seeded (pitted)* | *225 g* | *8 oz* | *1¹/₃ cups* |

1. Whisk the egg whites until stiff and fold into yoghurt.

2. Layer the yoghurt and most of the grapes into glasses and decorate with remaining grapes.

3. Chill until required.

Preparation time: 10 minutes plus chilling time

# Lemon and Honey Cheesecake

| Serves 4 | Metric | Imperial | American |
|---|---|---|---|
| *Eggs, separated* | 2 | 2 | 2 |
| *Half fat cottage cheese* | *225 g* | *8 oz* | *1 cup* |
| *Curd (smooth cottage) cheese* | *225 g* | *8 oz* | *1 cup* |
| *Clear honey* | *15 ml* | *1 tbsp* | *1 tbsp* |
| *Finely grated lemon rind* | *5 ml* | *1 tsp* | *1 tsp* |
| *Sultanas (golden raisins)* | *30 ml* | *2 tbsp* | *2 tbsp* |
| *Sweet Crumb Case (shell) (see page 127)* | *1 × 23 cm* | *1 × 9 in* | *1 × 9 in* |
| **To decorate:** | | | |
| *Thinly pared strips of lemon rind* | | | |

1. Whisk the egg whites until stiff. (If a recipe requires whisked egg whites, it is easier to do this first so you are using completely clean and dry utensils, otherwise the whites will not stiffen).

2. Beat together the cottage cheese, curd cheese, egg yolks, honey, lemon rind and sultanas.

3. Fold egg whites into mixture.

4. Pour on to biscuit base and bake for 30 minutes at 180°C/350°F/gas mark 4.

5. Cool, then chill. Decorate with strips of thinly pared lemon rind before serving.

Preparation time: 15 minutes
Cooking time: 30 minutes

# Lemon Tart

As an alternative to the Sweet Crumb Case in this recipe, you can use pastry case baked blind, made with 5 oz wholemeal flour (see pastry making, page 9).

| *F* Serves 4 | Metric | Imperial | American |
|---|---|---|---|
| *Sweet Crumb Case (shell) (see page 127) or cooked pastry (paste) case (shell)* | *1 × 18 cm* | *1 × 7 in* | *1 × 7 in* |
| *Sugar* | *75 g* | *3 oz* | *1/3 cup* |
| *Eggs* | *2* | *2* | *2* |
| *Juice and finely grated rind of lemon* | *1* | *1* | *1* |
| *Soya margarine, melted* | *25 g* | *1 oz* | *2 tbsp* |

1. Cook crumb case in oven at 180°C/350°F/gas mark 4 for 10 minutes.

2. Mix remaining ingredients together well and pour into cooked flan case.

3. Bake for 15 minutes.

4. Allow to cool before serving.

Preparation time: 15 minutes
Cooking time: 15 minutes

# Reduced Sugar Raspberry Pavlova

This is a fail–safe version of the ever-popular dessert and lower in calories than most recipes. Sprinkle with a few toasted sliced almonds. Pack in a rigid container if freezing, as meringue is inclined to be brittle when frozen.

| *F* Serves 4 | Metric | Imperial | American |
|---|---|---|---|
| *Case:* | | | |
| Egg whites | 3 | 3 | 3 |
| Vinegar | 1 tsp | 1 tsp | 1 tsp |
| Raw cane sugar | 50 g | 5 oz | ²/₃ cup |
| *Filling:* | | | |
| Quantity Cornmeal | | | |
| Custard (see page 149) | 1 | 1 | 1 |
| Raspberries | 150 g | 5 oz | ²/₃ cup |

1. Dampen a large baking sheet and cover with non-stick baking parchment.

2. Place the egg whites in a large bowl and whisk until stiff.

3. Add all the sugar and vinegar and continue whisking until mixture is very stiff.

4. Spread a circle of meringue on to the greaseproof paper and pipe or swirl the rest round the outside to make a nest shape.

5. Place in a cool oven, 150°C/300°F/gas mark 2 and immediately turn the heat down to 140°C/275°F/gas mark 1. Cook for 1 hour.

6. Turn the oven off and leave overnight to dry out completely. Peel off the paper.

7. Fill with the cool cornmeal custard and top with raspberries.

Preparation time: 15 minutes
Cooking time: 1 hour, plus drying out

# Rhubarb and Banana Fool

This recipe uses bananas to sweeten instead of sugar.

| *M* Serves 4 | Metric | Imperial | American |
|---|---|---|---|
| Rhubarb, cut into chunks | 450 g | 1 lb | 1 lb |
| Honey | 15 ml | 1 tbsp | 1 tbsp |
| Cinnamon | 5 ml | 1 tsp | 1 tsp |
| Ripe bananas, peeled and halved | 50 g | 1 lb | 1 lb |
| Low fat natural (plain) yoghurt | 300 ml | 1/2 pt | 1 1/4 cups |
| Toasted chopped hazelnuts | 50 g | 2 oz | 1/2 cup |

1. Put the rhubarb, honey, cinnamon and 45 ml/3 tbsp of cold water in a pan and stew gently until rhubarb is tender.

2. Cool slightly and place in a blender or food processor with the bananas. Run machine until mixture is smooth.

3. Leave until cold then fold in the yoghurt.

4. Turn into individual serving dishes and decorate with the hazelnuts. Chill if time allows before serving.

Preparation time: 15 minutes plus cooling and chilling time

# Sweet Crumb Case (Shell)

This is a very useful recipe to have to hand. It is much less time-consuming than pastry and can be cooked or used just as it is, once set. The quantity makes two 18 cm/7 in cases so one can be frozen for future use. Alternatively, use mixture to make one 23 cm/9 in case.

| *F* | Metric | Imperial | American |
|---|---|---|---|
| Crushed wholemeal digestive biscuits (graham crackers) (or any other plain, wholemeal variety) | 225 g | 8 oz | 2 cups |
| Soya margarine, melted | 75 g | 3 oz | 1/3 cup |
| Golden (light corn) syrup | 15 ml | 1 tbsp | 1 tbsp |
| Ground ginger | pinch | pinch | pinch |

1. Mix the biscuits into the melted margarine with the syrup and ginger and mix well.

2. Press into 2 x 18 cm/7 in greased flan dishes.

3. Chill for 2 hours to set.

4. Fill as desired (see other recipes in this section).

Preparation time: 10 minutes plus chilling time

# Vanilla Cheesecake

| Serves 4 | Metric | Imperial | American |
|---|---|---|---|
| *Sweet Crumb Case (shell)* | | | |
| *(see page 127)* | *1 × 23 cm* | *1 × 9 in* | *1 × 9 in* |
| *Half fat cottage cheese* | *350 g* | *12 oz* | *1¹/₂ cups* |
| *Eggs, beaten* | *2* | *2* | *2* |
| *Soured (dairy sour) cream* | *300 ml* | *¹/₂ pt* | *1¹/₄ cups* |
| *Real vanilla essence (extract)* | *5 ml* | *1 tsp* | *1 tsp* |
| *Sugar* | *50 g* | *2 oz* | *¹/₄ cup* |
| ***To decorate:*** | | | |
| *Fresh sliced fruits* | | | |

1. Bake crumb base for 10 minutes at 180°C/350°F/ gas mark 4.

2. Beat together the cottage cheese, eggs, sugar, soured cream and vanilla essence. Pour into base.

3. Return to oven for 30-35 minutes until set.

4. Cool then chill.

5. Decorate with sliced fresh fruits before serving.

Preparation time: 15 minutes plus chilling time
Cooking time: 40-45 minutes

# Winter Fruit Fool

For the sweet–toothed, this recipe is ideal, but it contains no sugar and the texture is absolutely delicious - like velvet. For a special occasion, use 300 ml/½ pt/1¼ cups whipped low fat cream instead of the custard.

| *F* Serves 4 | Metric | Imperial | American |
|---|---|---|---|
| *Quantity Winter Fruit Salad (see page 130)* | *1* | *1* | *1* |
| *Cornmeal Custard (see page 149)* | *300 ml* | *½ pt* | *1¼ cups* |
| **To decorate:** | | | |
| *Chopped toasted hazelnuts* | | | |

1. Purée Winter Fruit Salad in a blender or food processor for 2 minutes until smooth.

2. Add custard and continue to process for a further minute.

3. Serve in tall glasses and decorate with chopped, toasted hazelnuts.

Preparation time: 20 minutes plus soaking time

# Winning Ways with Fruit

What could be more tempting than being offered a beautiful selection of fresh fruit at the end of a meal? With a little imagination it needn't cost a lot to produce a mouth–watering selection of what is, after all, probably the best dessert there is. When assembling an arrangement of fruit, try to choose pieces that will give different textures, colours, shapes and sizes. Use a pretty bowl or basket to put them in with perhaps a few of their own leaves if possible. Always wash the fruit well beforehand.

**Fresh Fruit Salad** too is always welcome at the end of a meal and many variations can be made from the fruits available in your local supermarket or market. Buy a small can of fruit in natural juice and add 150 ml/$^1$/$_4$ pt/$^2$/$_3$ cup fresh orange juice, 5 ml/1 tsp lemon juice and a sprinkling of ground cinnamon as the base of your salad and fill up with washed, chopped fresh fruit. Leaving on any edible peel gives colour and texture and retains some of the goodness. A scooped–out pineapple or melon shell makes a perfect natural receptacle for fresh fruit salad, or use halved grapefruit or large orange shells for individual helpings.

Add 150 g/5 oz/1$^1$/$_4$ cups desiccated (shredded) coconut, soaked in 120 ml/4 fl oz/$^1$/$_2$ cup water for 30 minutes, then drained, for the delicious Southern States of America Fruit Salad recipe **Ambrosia**.

A hot **Winter Fruit Salad** makes a change when it's cold outside. Soak 225 g/8 oz/1$^1$/$_3$ cups dried fruit (e.g. apricots, peaches, prunes, figs, dates, apples, bananas) in a bowl in 300 ml/$^1$/$_2$ pt/1$^1$/$_4$ cups fresh orange juice overnight. Add a pinch of mixed (apple pie) spice, bring to the boil and simmer for 10 minutes. Add 50 g/2 oz/$^1$/$_2$ cup toasted, flaked almonds to decorate just before serving.

Alternatively, make a **Winter Fruit Crumble**. Add 50 g/2 oz/$^1$/$_2$ cup toasted, flaked almonds to 175 g/6 oz/1$^1$/$_2$ cups wholemeal (graham) flour and 75 g/3 oz/$^1$/$_3$ cup soya margarine, rubbed in together and mixed with 50 g/2 oz/$^1$/$_4$ cup demarara (light brown) sugar and sprinkle on top of the fruit. Place in a greased ovenproof dish. Bake at 200°C/400°F/gas mark 6 for 25 minutes.

# Ice Cream Toppings

Instead of serving ice cream with sweet syrupy toppings, try these ideas instead:

50 g/4 tbsp home–made mincemeat (or a top quality wholefood brand), melted in the microwave just long enough to be made pourable.

225 g/8 oz/1 cup frozen raspberries or other fruit puréed through a sieve, mixed with a little honey and poured over.

Heat 150 ml/$^1$/$_4$ pt/$^2$/$_3$ cup fresh orange juice and 1.5 ml/$^1$/$_4$ tsp raw cane syrup in the microwave on high for 2 minutes. Stir in 5 ml/1 tsp arrowroot dissolved in 15 ml/1 tbsp water and heat until thickened.

Dissolve 15 ml/1 tbsp carob powder in 150 ml/$^1$/$_4$ pt/$^2$/$_3$ cup black decaffeinated coffee. Add 2.5 ml/$^1$/$_2$ tsp raw cane sugar and heat gently in the microwave. Stir in 5 ml/1 tsp arrowroot dissolved in 15 ml/1 tbsp water and heat until thickened.

# CHAPTER 5

# BREADS, BISCUITS AND CAKES

In the following section you will find a selection of savoury breads to serve with soups, starters or main courses and tempting tea breads to fill the gap between lunch or supper as well as cakes and biscuits that are packed with goodness. A delicious assortment, I am sure you'll agree.

# Belgian Tea Loaf

| *F* Serves 4 | Metric | Imperial | American |
|---|---|---|---|
| *Teacup sultanas (golden raisins) or raisins* | 1 | 1 | 1 |
| *Same sized teacup skimmed milk* | 1 | 1 | 1 |
| *Same sized teacup demerara (light brown) sugar* | 1 | 1 | 1 |
| *Soya margarine* | 100 g | 4 oz | 1/2 cup |
| *Egg, beaten* | 1 | 1 | 1 |
| *Same sized teacups wholemeal (graham) self raising (self-rising) flour* | 2 | 2 | 2 |
| *Mixed (apple pie) spice* | pinch | pinch | pinch |
| *Salt* | pinch | pinch | pinch |
| *A little sugar for sprinkling* | | | |

1. Put the sultanas or raisins, milk, sugar and margarine into a saucepan and bring to the boil, stirring until margarine has melted.

2. Leave to cool slightly.

3. Beat in the egg, flour, spice and salt.

4. Pour into a greased 450 g/1 lb loaf tin, sprinkle with a little more demerara sugar and bake for one hour at 190°C/375°F/ gas mark 5. Turn out after 5 minutes on to a wire rack to cool.

5. Serve sliced, spread with soya margarine, if liked.

Preparation time: 10 minutes
Cooking time: 1 hour plus cooling time

# Celery and Cheese Loaf

| *F* Serves 4 | Metric | Imperial | American |
|---|---|---|---|
| Wholemeal (graham) self raising (self-rising) flour | 275 g | 10 oz | 2½ cups |
| Salt and pepper | | | |
| Soya margarine | 50 g | 2 oz | ¼ cup |
| Sticks (ribs) celery, chopped | 2 | 2 | 2 |
| Grated vegetarian Cheddar cheese | 100 g | 4 oz | 1 cup |
| Egg, beaten | 1 | 1 | 1 |
| Skimmed milk | 150 ml | ¼ pt | ⅔ cup |

1. Mix together the flour, salt, pepper, margarine, celery and cheese.

2. Add the egg and milk and mix to a soft dough.

3. Knead lightly in the bowl with floured hands.

4. Transfer to a greased 450 g/1 lb loaf tin.

5. Bake at 190°C/375°F/gas mark 5 for 1 hour.

6. Leave in the tin for 5 minutes, then turn out to cool on a wire rack. Serve warm or cold with soya or sunflower margarine.

Preparation time: 10 minutes
Cooking time: 1 hour

# Cheese 'Rolls'

These are delicious and make a change from ordinary bread rolls. Serve with soup or salads.

| Serves 4 | Metric | Imperial | American |
|---|---|---|---|
| *Slices of wholemeal bread, crusts removed* | *8* | *8* | *8* |
| *Soya margarine, melted* | *100 g* | *4 oz* | *¹/₂ cup* |
| *Grated vegetarian Cheddar cheese* | *75 g* | *3 oz* | *³/₄ cup* |
| *Paprika* | | | |

1. Flatten each slice of bread by rolling firmly with a rolling pin.

2. Brush each slice with melted margarine, sprinkle with cheese and paprika and roll up.

3. Place on a greased baking sheet and brush with margarine. Bake at 200°C/400°F/gas mark 6 for 10 minutes, then turn over.

4. Brush with remaining margarine and cook for a further 10 minutes until crisp and golden. Serve hot.

Preparation time: 5 minutes
Cooking time: 20 minutes

# Fruity Fibre Teacup Loaf

This sounds typically wholesomely boring! But I can assure you it is really moist and delicious, extremely easy to make and uses no fat. It improves with keeping.

| *F* Serves 4 | Metric | Imperial | American |
|---|---|---|---|
| *Teacup malted All Bran cereal* | *1* | *1* | *1* |
| *Same sized teacup demerara (light brown) sugar* | *1* | *1* | *1* |
| *Same sized teacup mixed dried fruit (fruit cake mix)* | *1* | *1* | *1* |
| *Same sized teacup skimmed milk* | *1* | *1* | *1* |
| *Same sized teacup wholemeal (graham) self raising (self-rising) flour* | *1* | *1* | *1* |
| *Mixed (apple pie) spice* | *pinch* | *pinch* | *pinch* |
| *Salt* | *pinch* | *pinch* | *pinch* |
| *A little extra sugar for topping* | | | |

1. Soak the cereal, sugar and mixed fruit in milk in a bowl for 1 hour.

2. Grease a 450g/1 lb loaf tin.

3. Add the flour, mixed spice and salt to mixture and combine well. Pour into tin, sprinkle the top with a little extra demerara sugar and cook for 1¼ hours at 180°C/350°F/gas mark 4.

4. Remove from oven, leave in tin for 5 minutes, then turn out on to a wire rack to cool.

5. Serve sliced and spread sparingly with soya margarine if liked.

**Variation:**
Substitute chopped ready-to-eat dried apricots for the mixed fruit, omit the spice and add 15 ml/1 tbsp clear honey.

Preparation time: 5 minutes plus soaking time
Cooking time: 1¼ hours

# Garlic Bread

| *F* Serves 4 | Metric | Imperial | American |
|---|---|---|---|
| Brown Vienna loaf | 1 | 1 | 1 |
| Garlic clove, crushed | 1 | 1 | 1 |
| OR garlic powder | 2.5 ml | ¹/₂ tsp | ¹/₂ tsp |
| Soya margarine | 50 g | 2 oz | ¹/₄ cup |
| Fresh chopped mixed herbs | 30 ml | 2 tbsp | 2 tbsp |
| OR dried mixed herbs (optional) | 7.5 ml | 1¹/₂ tsp | 1¹/₂ tsp |
| Salt and pepper | | | |
| Lemon juice | 2.5 ml | ¹/₂ tsp | ¹/₂ tsp |

1. Slice the loaf diagonally in 2 cm/¾ in slices.

2. Mix the crushed garlic or garlic powder with the margarine, mixed herbs, (if liked) salt, pepper and lemon juice.

3. Spread each slice of bread with the mixture.

4. Re–shape loaf and wrap in foil, sealing the ends firmly. Heat through in the oven at 200°C/400°F/gas mark 6 for 15 minutes.

5. Serve in a long bread basket still wrapped in the foil to keep it warm.

Preparation time: 8 minutes
Cooking time: 15 minutes

# Herby Baps

| *F* Serves 4 | Metric | Imperial | American |
|---|---|---|---|
| Brown baps, split in halves<br>A little soya margarine<br>Fresh, chopped or dried<br>   herbs | 4 | 4 | 4 |

1. Spread the baps with a little margarine and sprinkle with the mixed herbs.

2. Place under a hot grill (broiler) for 2 minutes until just browned. Serve with soup or light lunches.

Preparation time: 2 minutes
Cooking time: 2 minutes

# Carob Chews

It has recently been discovered that oats are extremely good for helping to reduce cholesterol. They make an excellent instant thickener for savoury dishes and can be used in many cake and biscuit recipes.

| *M* *F* Serves 4 | Metric | Imperial | American |
|---|---|---|---|
| Sugar | 50 g | 2 oz | $^{1}/_{4}$ cup |
| Golden (light corn) syrup or molasses | 30 ml | 2 tbsp | 2 tbsp |
| Soya margarine | 75 g | 3 oz | $^{1}/_{3}$ cup |
| Rolled oats | 225 g | 8 oz | 2 cups |
| Carob powder | 45 ml | 3 tbsp | 3 tbsp |
| Real vanilla or almond essence (extract) | 5 ml | 1 tsp | 1 tsp |
| Walnuts, chopped | 25 g | 1 oz | $^{1}/_{4}$ cup |
| Sultanas (golden raisins), chopped | 50 g | 2 oz | $^{1}/_{3}$ cup |

1. Put the sugar, syrup or molasses and margarine in a large pan and heat gently until margarine and sugar have melted.

2. Stir in the oats, carob powder, vanilla essence, walnuts and sultanas and mix well.

3. Press into a greased 25 × 16 cm/10 × 6 in shallow tin (pan). Chill to set for 3 hours.

4. Cut into 5 cm/2 in squares and serve.

Preparation time: 10 minutes plus chilling time.

# Crumble Cake

| *M* *F* Serves 4 | Metric | Imperial | American |
|---|---|---|---|
| Soya margarine | 50 g | 2 oz | 1/4 cup |
| Demerara (light brown) sugar | 25 g | 1 oz | 2 tbsp |
| Golden (light corn) syrup | 15 ml | 1 tbsp | 1 tbsp |
| Carob powder | 15 ml | 1 tbsp | 1 tbsp |
| Sultanas (golden raisins) | 45 ml | 3 tbsp | 3 tbsp |
| Natural almond essence (extract) | few drops | few drops | few drops |
| Wholemeal digestive biscuits (graham crackers), crushed | 225 g | 8 oz | 2 cups |

1. Put all ingredients, except biscuits, into a large pan and heat gently until margarine and sugar have melted.

2. Add biscuits and stir well.

3. Press into a greased 18 cm/7 in sandwich tin (pan) and chill overnight.

4. Turn out and cut into small portions as this is very rich.

Preparation time: 10 minutes plus chilling time

# Mincemeat Cake

This cake keeps well in an airtight tin.

| *F* Serves 4 | Metric | Imperial | American |
|---|---|---|---|
| Soya margarine | 100 g | 4 oz | 1/2 cup |
| Demerara (light brown) sugar | 100 g | 4 oz | 1/2 cup |
| Eggs, size 1 | 3 | 3 | 3 |
| Wholemeal (graham) self raising (self-rising) flour | 200 g | 7 oz | 1 3/4 cups |
| Vegetarian mincemeat | 350 g | 12 oz | 1 cup |
| Salt | pinch | pinch | pinch |
| Skimmed milk | 150 ml | 1/4 pt | 2/3 cup |

1. Beat the margarine, sugar and eggs together well.

2. Add the flour, mincemeat, salt and milk and continue beating until well blended.

3. Turn into a 20 cm/8 in round cake tin (pan) and bake at 160°C/325°F/gas mark 3 for 1¼ hours.

4. Leave in tin for 5 minutes, turn out and cool on a wire rack.

Preparation time: 10 minutes
Cooking time: 1¼ hours

# Oatmeal Shortbread

A good old–fashioned favourite, but made a lot easier with the aid of a food processor. I usually make two rounds up at a time. The oatmeal gives it an unusual texture.

| *F* Serves 4 | Metric | Imperial | American |
|---|---|---|---|
| *Wholemeal (graham) flour* | *175 g* | *6 oz* | *1½ cups* |
| *Caster (superfine) sugar* | *50 g* | *2 oz* | *¼ cup* |
| *Soya margarine* | *100 g* | *4 oz* | *½ cup* |
| *Medium oatmeal* | *25 g* | *1 oz* | *¼ cup* |
| *Salt* | *pinch* | *pinch* | *pinch* |

1. Put all ingredients into a food processor and process for 1 minute until a ball forms.

2. Tip into a greased 18 cm/7 in sandwich tin (pan) and press down well.

3. Mark into eight portions and prick all over with a fork.

4. Bake for 45 minutes at 160°C/325°F/gas mark 3 until pale golden in colour. Cool in the tin, then store in an airtight container.

Preparation time: 5 minutes
Cooking time: 45 minutes

# Orange and Carob Chip Cake

| *F* Serves 4 | Metric | Imperial | American |
|---|---|---|---|
| Soya margarine | 100 g | 4 oz | ½ cup |
| Sugar | 100 g | 4 oz | ½ cup |
| Eggs | 2 | 2 | 2 |
| Wholemeal (graham) self raising (self-rising) flour | 100 g | 4 oz | 1 cup |
| Carob chips | 75 g | 3 oz | ¾ cup |
| Chopped walnuts | 50 g | 2 oz | ½ cup |
| Fresh orange juice | 15 ml | 1 tbsp | 1 tbsp |
| Finely–grated orange rind | 10 ml | 2 tsp | 2 tsp |
| Lemon or orange curd (see page 151) | | | |

1. Put the margarine, sugar and orange peel in a bowl and beat together.

2. Beat in the eggs one at a time.

3. Fold in the flour with the carob chips, walnuts, orange juice and rind and mix well.

4. Turn into two 18 cm/7 in greased sandwich tins (pans) and bake for 25 minutes at 190°C/375°F/gas mark 5 until risen and centres spring back when lightly pressed.

5. Turn out on to a wire rack to cool.

6. Sandwich together with home-made lemon or orange curd.

Preparation time: 10 minutes plus cooling time
Cooking time: 25 minutes

# Swiss Cake

If your children won't eat breakfast - try giving them a slice of this nutritious cake with a glass of milk - unusual, but I bet they'll eat it.

| *F* Serves 4 | Metric | Imperial | American |
|---|---|---|---|
| *Unsweetened muesli* | *175 g* | *6 oz* | *1¹/₂ cups* |
| *Skimmed milk* | *150 ml* | *¹/₄ pt* | *²/₃ cup* |
| *Wholemeal (graham) self raising (self-rising) flour* | *175 g* | *6 oz* | *1¹/₂ cups* |
| *Demerara (light brown) sugar* | *185 g* | *6¹/₂ oz* | *good ³/₄ cup* |
| *Eggs, beaten* | *3* | *3* | *3* |

1. Place the muesli and milk in a bowl and leave to soak for 30 minutes.

2. Grease an 18 cm/7 in cake tin.

3. Mix the flour and 175 g/6 oz/¾ cup of sugar together.

4. Rub in the margarine, add eggs and muesli in milk and beat well.

5. Spoon into tin and smooth the surface.

6. Sprinkle with remaining sugar and bake in the oven at 180°C/350°F/gas mark 4 for 1¼ hours, until well risen and a skewer inserted in the centre comes out clean.

7. Leave in tin for 5 minutes, then turn out and leave to cool on a wire rack.

8. Store in an airtight tin.

Preparation time: 10 minutes plus soaking and cooling time
Cooking time: 1¼ hours

# Walnut Brownies

| *M* *F* Serves 4 | Metric | Imperial | American |
|---|---|---|---|
| Wholemeal (graham) flour | 50 g | 2 oz | 1/2 cup |
| Baking powder | pinch | pinch | pinch |
| Salt | 1.5 ml | 1/4 tsp | 1/4 tsp |
| Soya margarine | 75 g | 3 oz | 1/2 cup |
| Carob chips | 50 g | 2 oz | 1/2 cup |
| Demerara (light brown) sugar | 175 g | 6 oz | 3/4 cup |
| Eggs, beaten | 2 | 2 | 2 |
| Vanilla essence (extract) | 2.5 ml | 1/2 tsp | 1/2 tsp |
| Walnuts, chopped | 50 g | 2 oz | 1/2 cup |

1. Mix the flour, baking powder and salt together.

2. Melt the margarine and carob chips in bowl over pan of hot water (or in the microwave). Beat in the sugar, eggs and vanilla essence.

3. Stir into flour mixture with the walnuts.

4. Turn into a greased 18 x 28 cm/7 x 11 in baking tin (pan).

5. Bake at 180°C/350°F/gas mark 4 for 35 minutes. Cool in tin then cut into squares. Store in an airtight tin.

Preparation time: 10 minutes
Cooking time: 35 minutes

# Wheatflake Crackle Cakes

An all–time favourite with the children and one they can help you make too. Ring the changes with bran or oatbran flakes and different dried fruit.

| *M* Serves 4 | Metric | Imperial | American |
|---|---|---|---|
| *Soya margarine* | *25 g* | *1 oz* | *2 tbsp* |
| *Golden (light corn) syrup* | *15 ml* | *1 tbsp* | *1 tbsp* |
| *Carob powder* | *15 ml* | *1 tbsp* | *1 tbsp* |
| *Demerara (light brown) sugar* | *15 ml* | *1 tbsp* | *1 tbsp* |
| *Raisins* | *30 ml* | *2 tbsp* | *2 tbsp* |
| *Wheatflake breakfast cereal, lightly crushed* | *105 ml* | *7 tbsp* | *7 tbsp* |

1. Put the margarine, syrup, carob powder, sugar and raisins in a large saucepan and heat gently, stirring until margarine and sugar have melted.

2. Add the wheatflakes and coat thoroughly.

3. Put dessertspoonfuls into paper cases and chill to set for at least 2 hours.

4. Store in the fridge or in an airtight tin.

Preparation time: 15-20 minutes

CHAPTER 6

# SAUCES AND SUNDRIES

This chapter contains several very handy recipes that will form the basis of a lot of your new dishes. It includes a basic white sauce, fruit spread and chutney recipes, plus some drinks and even instructions on how to dry-roast peanuts.

Remember too, that left-over vegetarian food can be converted into so many different dishes – burgers, rissoles (using the food processor), soups, sauces (using the liquidiser), risottos, pasta dishes, vegetable stuffings, crumbles or potato-topped dishes, for example.

# Apple and Cinnamon Spread

Fruit spreads are obviously a nutritious substitute for sugary commercial jams, but they do not keep as long. Always store in the fridge and eat within a week if possible.

| *F* | Metric | Imperial | American |
|---|---|---|---|
| *Large eating (dessert) apples, peeled, cored and chopped* | *2* | *2* | *2* |
| *Chopped, stoned (pitted) dates* | *100 g* | *4 oz* | *²/₃ cup* |
| *Cinnamon* | *2.5 ml* | *¹/₂ tsp* | *¹/₂ tsp* |
| *Water* | *175 ml* | *6 fl oz* | *³/₄ cup* |

1. Place the apples, dates, cinnamon and water in a saucepan and cover.

2. Bring to the boil and cook for 15 minutes until soft.

3. Mash with a potato masher, re-cover and cool with the lid still on.

4. Transfer to a sealed container and store in the fridge.

Preparation time: 5 minutes plus cooling time
Cooking time: 15 minutes

# Cornmeal Custard

Serve this as a sauce or as a filling for flans or cakes.

| *M* | Metric | Imperial | American |
|---|---|---|---|
| Fine cornmeal (available from health food shops) | 15 ml | 1 tbsp | 1 tbsp |
| Sugar | 30 ml | 2 tbsp | 2 tbsp |
| Skimmed milk | 450 ml | ³/₄ pt | 2 cups |
| Natural vanilla essence (extract) | 2.5 ml | ¹/₂ tsp | ¹/₂ tsp |

1. Mix the cornmeal and sugar together and make a smooth paste with a little of the milk.

2. Heat the rest of the milk in a saucepan.

3. Pour on to the cornmeal paste, add the vanilla essence and return to the pan.

4. Bring to the boil and simmer for 5 minutes, stirring all the time.

Preparation time: 3 minutes
Cooking time: 7 minutes

# Easy White Sauce

This quantity makes 300 ml/½ pt/1¼ cups of sauce.

| *M* *F* | Metric | Imperial | American |
|---|---|---|---|
| Soya margarine | 25 g | 1 oz | 2 tbsp |
| Plain (all-purpose) flour | 25 g | 1 oz | ¼ cup |
| Salt and pepper | | | |
| Skimmed milk | 300 ml | ½ pt | 1¼ cups |

1. Put all ingredients in a saucepan and whisk until flour is well blended.

2. Bring to the boil, whisking all the time and simmer for 2 minutes. Use as required.

Preparation time: 3 minutes
Cooking time: 4 minutes

# Lemon or Orange Curd

| *F* | Metric | Imperial | American |
|---|---|---|---|
| Lemons<br>  OR | 2-3 | 2-3 | 2-3 |
| Oranges | 1-2 | 1-2 | 1-2 |
| Soya margarine | 100 g | 4 oz | ½ cup |
| Sugar | 225 g | 8 oz | 1 cup |
| Eggs, beaten | 2 | 2 | 2 |

1. Pare the rind from the fruit thinly. Squeeze and strain the juice.

2. Melt the soya margarine in a bowl over a pan of hot water.

3. Whisk in the sugar, rind, juice and the eggs.

4. Continue cooking over a gentle heat, stirring occasionally, until mixture thickens and coats the back of a spoon.

5. Strain into clean jars, cover, label and store in a cool dark place.

Preparation time: 10 minutes
Cooking time: 15-20 minutes

# Mayonnaise

Unfortunately, there is just no quick way to make successful mayonnaise (I know, I've tried them all!). It is time–consuming, but well worth the effort. Alternatively, use a good quality commercial variety - but not salad cream.

|  | **Metric** | **Imperial** | **American** |
|---|---|---|---|
| *Egg yolks* | *2* | *2* | *2* |
| *Mustard powder* | *2.5 ml* | *¹/₂ tsp* | *¹/₂ tsp* |
| *Salt* | *2.5 ml* | *¹/₂ tsp* | *¹/₂ tsp* |
| *Sugar* | *2.5 ml* | *¹/₂ tsp* | *¹/₂ tsp* |
| *Worcestershire sauce* | *1.5 ml* | *¹/₄ tsp* | *¹/₄ tsp* |
| *Pepper* | *pinch* | *pinch* | *pinch* |
| *Soya or olive oil* | *300 ml* | *¹/₂ pt* | *1¹/₄ cups* |
| *Vinegar* | *30 ml* | *2 tbsp* | *2 tbsp* |
| *Hot water* | *15 ml* | *1 tbsp* | *1 tbsp* |

1. Put the yolks, mustard, salt, sugar, Worcestershire sauce and pepper into a bowl and beat with an electric mixer until smooth (or liquidise in a blender goblet for 15-20 seconds).

2. Add half the oil, a drop at a time, and continue beating until mixture is thick.

3. Stir in half the vinegar.

4. Continue beating in oil gradually.

5. Add remaining vinegar and the hot water.

6. Put in a covered container. Store in the fridge for up to 2 weeks.

Preparation time: 10-15 minutes

# Processor Chutney

This is the easiest Chutney recipe I know and the food processor makes it even easier. It keeps well, makes an ideal gift for friends and is a tasty addition to sandwiches or curries.

|  | **Metric** | **Imperial** | **American** |
|---|---|---|---|
| *Cooking (tart) apples, cored and quartered* | *450 g* | *1 lb* | *1 lb* |
| *Onions, quartered* | *450 g* | *1 lb* | *1 lb* |
| *Demerara (light brown) sugar* | *450 g* | *1 lb* | *2 cups* |
| *Sultanas (golden raisins)* | *450 g* | *1 lb* | *2²/₃ cups* |
| *Dates, stoned (pitted) and chopped* | *450 g* | *1 lb* | *2²/₃ cups* |
| *Vinegar* | *600 ml* | *1 pt* | *2¹/₂ cups* |
| *Salt and pepper* |  |  |  |
| *Cayenne pepper* | *2.5 ml* | *¹/₂ tsp* | *¹/₂ tsp* |
| *Allspice powder* | *2.5 ml* | *¹/₂ tsp* | *¹/₂ tsp* |
| *Ground ginger* | *2.5 ml* | *¹/₂ tsp* | *¹/₂ tsp* |

1. Place the apples and onions in food processor and process for 1 minute or until finely chopped. Alternatively, pass through a coarse mincer (grinder).

2. Put all ingredients into a large bowl, stir well and cover. Leave for 24 hours, stirring occasionally.

3. Bottle and label. Store in a cool, dark place.

Preparation time: 10 minutes, plus standing time

# Sweetmeats

Even the most health–conscious of us needn't go without! These delicious morsels are a treat any time, but look especially pretty in *petit four* cases for Christmas or at other festivities throughout the year. All these recipes freeze well so can be made a long time ahead.

# Carob-Coated Nuts

Melt 225 g/8 oz/2 cups carob chips and dip whole brazil nuts, walnuts, almonds, peanuts, etc. into it (tweezers or fine tongs help considerably!). Transfer to greaseproof paper to set.

# Stuffed Dates

Remove the stones (pits) from fresh dates and fill with either a whole walnut, almond, a piece of fresh pineapple, mandarin segment or other fresh fruit, or a small piece of freshly–made almond paste. These dates are not freezable when stuffed with fresh fruit.

# Nut Clusters

| *M* *F* | Metric | Imperial | American |
|---|---|---|---|
| Carob chips | 100 g | 4 oz | 1 cup |
| Mixed chopped nuts | 100 g | 4 oz | 1 cup |
| Raisins, glacé (candied) cherries or sultanas (golden raisins) | 25 g | 1 oz | 2 tbsp |

1. Melt the carob chips in a pan over hot water or in the microwave. Cool slightly and stir in the nuts and raisins. Place teaspoonfuls on to greaseproof paper and leave to harden.

Preparation time: 5 minutes

# Dry Roasted Peanuts or other nuts

Put about 45 ml/3 tbsp of raw peanuts on a piece of kitchen paper into the microwave and spread out in a ring to prevent the middle ones burning. Microwave on high for 3-4 minutes or until golden brown. Cool, store in a screw-topped jar and use as a topping for curries, to serve with drinks or just to add to the older children's lunch boxes.

For a more savoury taste, microwave on a plate and sprinkle 30 ml/2 tbsp of soy sauce over the peanuts for the last minute of cooking.

Preparation time: 5 minutes

# Lemon Barley Water

A very refreshing drink in the summer and probably more popular with the adults than the children, especially at Wimbledon time!

|  | Metric | Imperial | American |
|---|---|---|---|
| *Pearl barley* | *50 g* | *2 oz* | *good ¹/₄ cup* |
| *Demerara (light brown) sugar* | *50 g* | *2 oz* | *¹/₄ cup* |
| *Juice of large lemons, strained* | *2* | *2* | *2* |

1. Put the barley into a saucepan, just cover with cold water and bring to the boil.

2. Drain and rinse the barley under cold running water.

3. Return the barley to the saucepan, add 600 ml/1 pt/2½ cups cold water and bring to the boil again.

4. Cover and simmer for 1 hour.

5. Strain the liquid into a jug or basin, stir in the sugar and cool.

6. When the mixture is cold, add the strained lemon juice. Dilute to serve. Store in the fridge.

Preparation time: 5 minutes plus cooling time
Cooking time: 1 hour 5 minutes

# Milk Shakes

Always a children's favourite! However these needn't necessarily be made with sickly, artificially-coloured syrups, and chemically-filled ice creams.

|  | Metric | Imperial | American |
|---|---|---|---|
| *Ice-cold skimmed milk* | *250 ml* | *8 fl oz* | *1 cup* |
| ***Flavour with any*** | | | |
| ***of the following:*** | | | |
| *Ripe banana* | *1* | *1* | *1* |
| *Carob powder* | *15 ml* | *1 tbsp* | *1 tbsp* |
| *A little fresh fruit purée* | | | |
| *Honey* | *5 ml* | *1 tsp* | *1 tsp* |

1. Put the milk and chosen flavouring into a blender or liquidiser and run the machine for about 1 minute.

2. Serve with a colourful straw in a tall glass to make the froth last longer.

Preparation time: 2 minutes

# Orange Cordial

Although it contains sugar, this cordial is not as sweet as commercially-made squashes or fizzy drinks and contains no preservatives. It keeps well in the fridge for up to 3 weeks and should be diluted in the same proportions as orange squash. Add carbonated water for sparkle.

| *M* | Metric | Imperial | American |
|---|---|---|---|
| *Boiling water* | *900 ml* | *1½ pts* | *3¾ cups* |
| *Sugar* | *225 g* | *8 oz* | *1 cup* |
| *Oranges, scrubbed* | *3* | *3* | *3* |
| *Citric acid* | *5 ml* | *1 tsp* | *1 tsp* |

1. Pour the boiling water over the sugar in a pan. Heat gently, stirring until sugar has completely dissolved.

2. Remove from the heat, squeeze in the juice from the oranges, then chop up the skin and flesh and add these too.

3. Stir in the citric acid. Leave to cool, stirring occasionally.

4. Strain and bottle when completely cold.

Preparation time: 10 minutes plus cooling time

# INDEX